Creative

Crewel

Embroidery

Creative Crewel Embroidery

Traditions and Innovations

Judy Jeroy

Lark Books
A Division of Sterling Publishing Co., Inc.,
New York

Editors: Carol Parks, Dawn Cusick
Art Director: Elaine Thompson
Photographer: Evan Bracken, Light Reflections
Illustrator: Bernadette Wolf
Production Assistant: Hannes Charen
Editorial Assistants: Heather S. Smith, Catherine Sutherland
Front Cover Art: Inset, Judy Jeroy; background, Jan Kozicki

Library of Congress Cataloging-in-Publication Data
Jeroy, Judy.
    Creative crewel embroidery : traditions & innovations /
Judy Jeroy.
      p. cm.
    Includes index.
    ISBN 1-57990-187-5 (paperback)
    1. Crewelwork. I. Title.
  TT778.C7J47   1998
  746.44'6–dc21   98-26918
                                CIP

10 9 8 7 6 5 4 3

Published by Lark Books, a division of
Sterling Publishing Co., Inc.
387 Park Avenue South, New York, N.Y. 10016

Distributed in Canada by Sterling Publishing,
c/o Canadian Manda Group, One Atlantic Ave., Suite 105
Toronto, Ontario, Canada M6K 3E7

Distributed in the U.K. by:
Guild of Master Craftsman Publications Ltd.
Castle Place, 166 High Street, Lewes East Sussex, England BN7 1XU
Tel: (+ 44) 1273 477374, Fax: (+ 44) 1273 478606,
Email: pubs@thegmcgroup.com, Web: www.gmcpublications.com

Distributed in Australia by Capricorn Link (Australia) Pty Ltd., P.O. Box 704,
Windsor, NSW 2756 Australia

If you have questions or comments about this book, please contact:
Lark Books
67 Broadway
Asheville, NC 28801
(828) 236-9730
Printed in China

ISBN 1-57990-187-5

CONTENTS

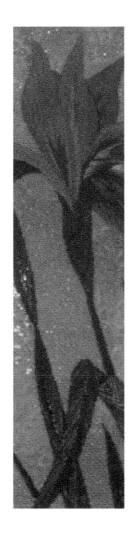

Environs: The View from my Window, by author Judy Jeroy.

INTRODUCTION

I never learned to embroider at the knee of my grandmother.

Rather, I entertained myself in 1955 with a commercial purchase of a set of stamped pillowcases. I taught myself to stitch following the directions given with the kit. Somehow, no matter how hard I tried, the results were less than satisfactory. The stem stitches didn't cover the stem line, the buttonhole stitches were wobbly, and the long and short stitches had dimples and uneven color distribution. I knew something was wrong but had no clue as to the solution or, indeed, the actual problem. Through the years, I repeated my mistakes, buying commercial kits and trying to stitch with less than satisfactory results. In 1974 I met Mary-Dick Digges and *my whole life changed*.

Mary-Dick taught a class in crewel embroidery at a monthly chapter meeting of The Embroiderers' Guild of America, Inc. I remember distinctly the design of a Christmas poinsettia, worked in Appleton crewel wools on cream linen twill. Having never before experienced the quality of materials nor the excellence of technique presented at that class, when I viewed my results under her tutelage, I was thrilled and amazed. No matter what the good intentions are, shoddy materials and inaccurate instruction most often produce poor results. I will be eternally grateful for the introduction into the world of crewel embroidery by Mary-Dick.

In the years since then I have studied with many prominent teachers. Two teachers who also had a profound impact on my crewel embroidery education are Audrey Francini and Betsy Leiper. They are both artists in their own right and have the ability to bring out astounding results in their students. Many of those featured here have studied with Mary-Dick, Audrey, or Betsy. I am sincerely grateful to those needle artists who responded so generously to my call for examples of their work. They are artists, one and all.

The opportunities available to me as a seeker after knowledge have almost invariably come from association with The Embroiderers' Guild of America, Inc., Suite 100, 335 West Broadway, Louisville, KY 40202. EGA's purpose is to foster the highest standards of excellence in the practice of the art of embroidery through an active program of education and study, and to preserve the heritage of the art of embroidery. They achieve this through a national network of more than 350 chapters and guilds. Most of my embroidery education has come through the auspices of EGA.

My studio is a long, wide room with lots of windows and skylights, which serve to illuminate the incredible mess within. My family is long suffering and patient with my avocation, encouraging me when I seem to take on too many projects and complimenting me when somehow I finish one.

This piece is a fragment of English crewel from the 18th century. The difference in the fabric color occurred because the piece was used in a way that exposed part of it to light and left part of it protected. From the private collection of Mary-Dick Digges.

AN
ABBREVIATED
HISTORY

Embroidery is the art of ornamenting textiles, fabrics, and other materials with needlework. It is a method of decorating by sewing on a finished piece of cloth, which differentiates it from ornamentation woven into the fabric. Embroidery can decorate a surface, create a pattern of holes in a fabric, or trim an edge with stitches. Crewel embroidery is a form of ornamental needlework that is done with wool on a closely woven ground fabric. The word "crewel" actually refers to the type of wool used: a worsted yarn of two twisted strands, either finely spun or coarse. Like other forms of embroidery, crewel work has suffered from, and been subjected to, the whims of fashion, the tribulations of war, and the scarcity of time and materials. Interest in this art form, however, has at no time been wholly extinguished.

How did stitching start? Probably with a wet and shivering prehistoric woman who decided it was too difficult to keep picking up two or three small animal pelts that kept sliding off her shoulders. Since two skins give more coverage than one, they were probably joined with thorns or bone splinters. This experiment worked, and led to another: piercing the pelts made it possible to lace them together with sinews or vines. Long days and nights by the fire probably led to experimentation with pattern stitches for joining together the skins and hides, which could have inspired the attachment of bones and shells as ornaments. Through this long development, the sinews and vines gave way to strands of spun wool, and thread was used in its own right to beautify fabrics. Embroidery had been born.

In the ancient homes of Stone Age Lake Dwellers in Switzerland and northern Italy, investigation uncovered woven and plaited fabrics of flax, bast, (a woody fiber), and wool. This proved that very early humanity had learned the important skill of twisting fibers together to make a continuous long thread. Simple weaving had existed long before this twisting or spinning, but the natural length of a fiber limited its use. When a woman learned to lengthen fibers artificially, she acquired the ability to make clothes that would better protect the members of the tribe, allowing the tribe to survive longer.

Crewel work as a specific form began to flourish in England in the 16th and early 17th centuries. It was about then that the modern steel needle was probably introduced into England from China. By 1545 needles were being manufactured in England.

The Renaissance led to the revival of cultural activities, and attention turned to embroidery as an art. This new and widespread enthusiasm for ornament and display in dress and furnishings caused many women to devote their leisure to this art, offering both decorative results and an agreeable social pastime. At the beginning of this movement there were no printed patterns for needlework; needlewomen made and exchanged their own embroidered designs. In order to maintain their repertoire of stitches, they worked cloth memoranda or samplers. The finished samplers were carefully kept, and there are even records of them being bequeathed in wills.

The demand for patterns was exploited commercially, and in the 16th century the first printed pattern book for needlework was published. The introduction of pattern books resulted in all sorts of designs and motifs circulating throughout Europe. English editions of such compilations include *A Scholehouse for the Needle* (1624) and *The Needle's Excellency* (1634).

In the Elizabethan period the surge of interest in domestic embroidery reached a peak, and the work of amateurs became as important as that of professionals. Often a well-to-do household would employ a professional embroiderer to direct the work of the daughters of the home, even though the bulk of the work would be done by the mistress of the house and her maids.

The Elizabethan tradition of embroidery continued to flourish during the first quarter of the 17th century. Work of the mid and late 17th century exhibits evidence of Oriental and Near Eastern influence on English embroidery design. Some interesting applications of crewel embroidery of this period were large curtains worked on twilled linen with bold designs incorporating intertwined branches or stems, large curled leaves with notched edges, exotic flowers, and to a lesser degree, exotic animals. The recurring tree of life theme seemed to abound, with fernlike foliage, a restrained use of color, compactly filled backgrounds, and simple stitches.

Interest in the stitching of crewel work had by this time crossed the ocean, and the American tradition in crewel wools had begun. In due course American embroiderers were to develop their own recognizably national patterns and their own way of working.

When they packed for their new lives across the Atlantic, the ardent Puritan needleworkers most certainly included crewel wools, a selection of patterns, and appropriate fabric, in spite of the limited baggage space.

Once they arrived, however, the new settlers had little time for leisure pursuits and few materials to spare. The women nonetheless kept their memories of beautifully embroidered clothes and linens.

In 1630 a fleet of ships arrived to form the Massachusetts Bay Colony, bringing sheep from whose wool embroidery thread was soon made. Before long many women knew how to spin and weave, and almost every family grew flax from which

linen could be made. Through hard labor and the natural purifying process of pounding, combing, and bleaching, they made long-wearing linen fabric that grew whiter and softer with use. Conditions in the New World made it difficult for even the affluent to acquire basic supplies from Europe, but by the middle of the 17th century the colonies had grown so wealthy and self-reliant that England became alarmed that trade would decline. America, in its homespun period, was built upon the family unit, which gained its living by its own labor and resources and was accustomed to thinking and acting independently.

The colonial housewife also had to be a proficient amateur chemist. To color her yarn and fabric, she had to experiment with various lichens and wild flowers and perhaps lean on the lore of Native Americans to fill in her chromatic scale. While she had plenty of blues and browns and yellows, greens were elusive, and reds were scarce until cochineal was introduced. With the manifold tasks of daily living, it is a wonder that colonial women had any time for thought of decorating the textiles they had created.

Whenever a colonial woman sat down to rest, almost immediately she would reach into her "pocket" to retrieve her embroidery, crocheting, or tatting. This pocket is described as an apronlike container made of two fabric layers with a slit opening, bound together along the side and lower edge. The pocket was worn around the waist, hidden under the folds of the overskirt, its front perhaps decorated with embroidery. See page 87 for a modern example.

Over the generations, the English pattern tradition brought by the American settlers developed into a style with its own characteristic appearance. The lighter, more open designs used less wool, which was still scarce in the colonies. Indigenous plants and animals were depicted, as were scenes reflecting the new way of life in the young country. The chief difference between the American designs and the imported ones was simplicity. There was more space, an elimination of foliage, and a limited stitch vocabulary, so that what elaboration there was became far more obvious. It is unusual to find more than five or six different stitches used in any one piece of American crewel work, and many times a complete set of bed hangings was worked in only two or three.

This piece was designed and stitched by Mary-Dick Digges using motifs and stitches typical of 18th-century American crewel. The red was dyed with cochineal using a tin mordant.

THIS CREWEL PIECE WAS STITCHED IN THE 1940S BY MARGARET PARSHALL, ONE OF THE ORIGINAL MEMBERS OF THE AMERICAN BRANCH OF THE EMBROIDER'S GUILD IN ENGLAND. IN 1958, MARGARET SERVED AS FOUNDING PRESIDENT OF THE EMBROIDERERS' GUILD OF AMERICA, INC.

A crewel revival in the late 19th century saw the founding in 1879 of the Needlework School of the Museum of Fine Arts in Boston. The school made one of the first organized efforts to bring the art of needlework out of the doldrums into which it had fallen in the early Victorian period. The founding of the Society of Blue and White Needlework in Deerfield, Massachusetts, in 1896 was also an important event for the cause of needlework. The society was dedicated to the study, preservation, and revival of a truly American form, and gave expression to a new enthusiasm.

For 150 years the Industrial Revolution developed, moving through the Victorian era, a minor depression, World War I, a major depression, and World War II. During this time embroidery was carefully folded and stored, to remain untouched until the late 1950s when women again sought self expression through the needle. From this interim period came a few notable embroideries and stitchers. One such stitcher is Mariska Karacz, who came to America from Hungary at the end of World War I. She first studied dress designing, but then diverted her talents to embroidery. Her embroideries were unique in their original approach, with theme and subject achieving dominance over working method and technical skill.

Many organizations have been born out of the necessity for an exchange of ideas between needlewomen. Among them are The Embroiderers' Guild of America, Inc., the American Needlepoint Guild, and the National Standards Council of American Embroiderers (later known as Council of American Embroiderers), which disbanded in 1995.

Crewel embroidery as it is practiced today is still evolving, as it should be. In an article (Fall, 1975) for *Needle Arts*, the quarterly magazine of The Embroiderers' Guild of America, Joan Edwards states that "Another generation of embroiderers does not necessarily perpetuate unchanged the style it inherits." What was true in 1975 is even more applicable today. A new generation of stitchers has been taught the technique, but these stitchers reserve the right to handle design in their own ways. "Contemporary" can be defined as being of the time—that which is modern or timely. It does not always mean abstract or nonrealistic. An abstract design may be contemporary, but a contemporary piece is not necessarily abstract.

Preserving and studying the old traditions is fundamental and crucial, for without them we would have no sense of history and continuity. Many embroiderers today enjoy the execution of traditional stitches and have perfected the skills and techniques necessary to reproduce exquisite examples of historical designs. Other stitchers wish to explore the vast array of new threads and fabrics now available on the commercial market. They have painted and dyed their background fabrics; they have distressed, pleated, and applied fabrics onto the backgrounds; they have machine stitched layers on the ground fabric and then embellished it with hand stitching. Then there are those who have pushed the edges of embroidery so that only the stitches are the same as in crewel work, but the threads and fabrics are neither wool nor linen, and the designs are a far cry from the tree of life or the botanically impossible bouquet. All of these stitchers were inspired initially by crewel embroidery. They have taken care to learn the methods of correct technique, then have taken their knowledge with them as they explored the realm of What Might Be Possible with a bit of daring and inspiration.

The popular choice of objects to be embroidered has changed throughout the centuries, but the basic warmth and beauty of crewel embroidery and its offspring are as much appreciated today as in the past, and it continues to be a most satisfying outlet for self expression. ✳

An assortment of background fabrics (linens, monk's cloth, and printed fabric), threads (wool, silk, chenille, and blends), needles and hoops.

TOOLS AND TECHNIQUES

To stitch crewel embroidery one only needs fabric, a needle, and something to use as thread. Taking tools a step beyond the essentials, then, I suppose an easy chair can qualify as a "tool" if it enables the stitcher to pursue her art with more diligence and ease. Certainly, being able to see clearly is imperative, so better-than-adequate light is an important tool. Some stitchers find it relaxing to stitch with the television set on; glancing up from one's work to view the t.v. serves to exercise the eyes and reduce fatigue. Others prefer to listen to their favorite music, while others require absolute silence.

Fabric

Any number of fabrics can be found to support crewel embroidery or innovative surface stitchery, such as denim, wool, gabardine, sailcloth, and various twilled fabrics. We must not forget to allow "form to fit function"—that is, an embroidered footstool should be made of a very sturdy fabric, while an elegant picture may be stitched on silk. The important element of any fabric choice must be that it is of a very tight weave to allow for an infinite number of possibilities for needle placement. It is also important to practice stitching on a new fabric to determine if it will maintain the appropriate tension.

Linen twill is the preferred fabric for traditional crewel embroidery as it allows the greatest latitude for stitch placement. It has a very tight weave with a slight grain; the side with the stronger twill pattern is the right side. Other tightly woven cottons, linens, and upholstery satin all offer variations in texture and are suitable for crewel work. You may want to practice stitches on a scrap piece of fabric or "doodle" cloth.

Yarn and Thread

The preferred thread for traditional crewel is a two-ply twisted wool. It comes in a variety of sizes, from very fine Medici, through Appleton crewel wools (available in more than 300 colors and values), to the heavier Persian yarns. It is also acceptable to use other types of threads, such as linen, cotton, and synthetics.

The materials some artists use as thread can vary from thin slices of leather to ribbons, boucle yarn, chenille thread, rope, twine, and any number of synthetic threads and yarns. A wonderful array of new threads and yarns have been made from silk, rayon, polyester, nylon, and other synthetics.

In addition, many natural fiber threads have been further embellished by overdyes so that the same thread may have several colors along one length. The threads that will work well with crewel embroidery or innovative surface stitchery will vary with the particular stitch used. Chenille and boucle threads can work when woven or stitched over spokes or bars placed with a different, smoother, firmer thread. Rayon threads make wonderful bullion knots. Silk threads allow satin stitch to shine as nothing else. The stitch determines which thread to use.

Working with wool yarn requires special considerations. All wool yarn has a grain, or nap; it is smooth in one direction and rough in the other. Stitching with the smooth nap direction passing through the fabric allows the wool to lie more smoothly, with less wear on the yarn and fewer "hairs." To determine the nap direction of a piece of wool yarn, gently pass it through two fingers, first in one direction and then in the other. Doing this several times with the eyes closed enables you to discern the nap direction, however faintly. Go with your first instinct. When stitching, use a piece of yarn not longer than 15 to 18 inches (38 to 46 cm).

Needles

Chenille needles are preferable to the so-called crewel needles. With a longer eye and smaller shank, the chenille needle makes a smaller hole in the fabric. The chosen needle must be easy to thread and must make a hole in the fabric large enough for the yarn to pass through without undue stress.

Chenille needles come in various sizes. The larger the number, the smaller the needle. Numbers 20, 22, 24, and 26 are used with crewel wools such as Elsa Williams/Paternan Crewel, Appleton, and Medici, respectively.

Hoops and Frames

Crewel embroidery, as well as the innovative changes to it, can be worked in the hand or in a round, screw-adjustable hoop. It depends on the tension achieved by the individual stitcher. Some stitchers can work quite nicely with the fabric soft in their hand; others want or need the fabric to be stretched within a hoop. Indeed, some stitches are much easier to control with the fabric within a hoop, while others are easier to stitch soft in the hand.

A frame or hoop keeps the fabric smooth and taut during stitching. Generally, the finished work will reflect poor tension and poor stitch placement when no hoop is used, although certain line stitches can be worked in

the hand. If you want or need to use a hoop, choose an adjustable wooden or plastic hoop that has a screw for tightening. (Metal hoops can leave smudge marks on the fabric.) The use of a standing hoop or table clamp lets you use both hands for thread handling and lets you achieve a better result on stitches such as the French knots and bullion knots.

CREATING ORIGINAL DESIGNS WHEN YOU'RE NOT A PROFESSIONAL ARTIST IS MUCH EASIER WHEN YOU STUDY MAGAZINES AND OBJECTS FOR INSPIRATION.

Inspiration and Design

The mechanics and materials currently available allow you to go beyond the limits of drawing and painting into the tactile interpretation of a design. It is this stretch beyond the two-dimensional, while still maintaining your original vision and level of artistic excellence, that enables fine needlework to take its place as an art form.

When I am unable to achieve the perfect shape for a particular design motif, I resort to my filing system. I have folders labeled "Mammals," "Insects," "Birds," "Reptiles," and "Landscapes." In the folders I keep photographs that I've taken myself, as well as pages torn from such magazines as *Ranger Rick*, *Wild*

Bird, National Geographic, and the like. If I need a fountain, or a garden, or a goat, or an orchid, I go to the files and dig through them. I draw the shape I need using the pictures as inspiration.

The process of designing is an intricate and often painful one, and the artist spends many hours achieving and perfecting a worthy design. For some artists every stitch and color is planned in exquisite detail before work is begun. Others use a minimal sketch or thought to inspire them, preferring to design with threaded needle, ripping out and restitching as necessary. The sources of design are as varied as the process, with some inspired by works within a classical museum and others using sketches taken during a nature walk. Each work is as individual as a fingerprint. When you undertake to compose your first original design, you will discover the hidden creativity and the means to express the design ideas held within yourself. I wish you much joy in exploration!

Transferring Designs

Working from either tracing paper or directly from the pattern, center the design on the fabric, right side up. Secure the design paper to the fabric along one edge with a few pins or pieces of masking tape to hold it steady. It is very important *not* to pin the graphite carbon paper to the fabric as the pin holes will be marked by the carbon.

Lift the design and slip a piece of graphite carbon paper (found in art supply stores) between design and fabric. Be careful not to slide the carbon as it may smudge the fabric. Tape the free side down with masking tape. With a blunt, hard pencil or empty ballpoint pen, trace a few elements of the design. Lift carefully to check that the design is being transferred, then finish tracing.

Remember that *all* traced lines must be covered by embroidery.

Getting Started

If the fabric will be used for clothing, care should be taken to preshrink the fabric by washing it first before embroidery is started. Launder the fabric in the same manner as the garment will be laundered. In all cases, finish the raw edges of the fabric by hand whipping, by machine attaching a ¼-inch hem, by zigzag stitching, or by serging the edges to prevent ravelling.

Tying In, Ending Off, and Changing Yarn

Refrain from using knots when working crewel embroidery. They come undone, wear off, or leave lumps in the surface of your work. To tie in, on the back of the work in a place which will be covered by embroidery on the surface, take a tiny stitch as shown, catching a few threads of the back surface only. Pull through, leaving an ⅟₁₆ inch (2 mm) tail. Then take another stitch directly over this one but at a right angle to it, splitting the yarn of the first stitch. This should give a firm anchor with no noticeable bulge.

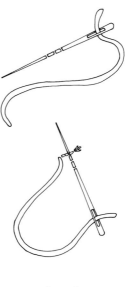

When ending off, run the needle through to the back, catch several threads of the twill, and take a few back stitches. Clip the thread ¹⁄₁₆ inch (2 mm) from the fabric.

Change yarns when the wool becomes weary or excessively hairy. The latter may indicate that you have threaded the needle against the grain or nap.

A Note on Signing Your Work

At least some of your stitched pieces will please you enough that you will wish to sign them. Keep in mind that the signature *will* become part of the design, and plan its addition carefully.

To sign my own work, I have chosen a simple device consisting of three Js (for Judith Jablonski Jeroy), all joined at the top without a crossbar, so that it looks like a trefoil design. I work it in simple back stitch, as small as I can get it, in a color to blend with the design. I like to tuck the signature into an inconspicuous place. Another way to make the signature disappear is to work it in thread that matches the background fabric; DMC color #712 is the same as the cream linen twill that I use.

Take a few minutes and experiment with pencil on paper. Try different arrangements of your initials, joining them in some manner. Simplify the initials by eliminating curves, blocking out the letters as if you were using back stitch. If you prefer to have a name in cursive writing, whipped back stitch with a few strands of six-strand cotton thread makes the finest, thinnest line.

If you wish to stitch a date on the front of the work, ensure that it is even less conspicuous than your initials. As we approach a new century, it might be appropriate to date the work using all the numbers for the year—e.g., "1999" rather than "'99." I seldom date my own work on the front, preferring instead to place a scrap of paper in the back of a piece, relating the date it was worked and with which materials.

Washing and Blocking

If the completed work is not dirty, it can be laced onto wooden stretcher strips and then rinsed. Assemble the stretcher strips into a frame that is at least 2 inches (5 cm) larger all around the piece. Lace with quilting thread, working from the center to the corners on each side. Tighten the lacing before knotting it. Then simply run the piece under the cold water faucet for a rinse. Let the water drain away, then dry the wooden strips thoroughly. Lay the piece flat for several days to dry completely.

If the work is soiled, lace it to stretcher strips as above. Wash it in tepid water with Ivory soap or Orvus (a commercial [livestock] shampoo). Dunk the piece in the suds, but do not wring or twist it. Rinse until you could *drink* the final rinse water, then dry it as described above.

Embroidery never should be ironed. Pressing can flatten or distort the stitched areas.

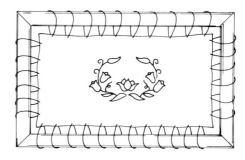

Mounting and Framing

Cut a piece of acid-free museum board or foam core to fit the frame. Smooth the edges, or cover the board with a piece of flannel. Center the work on the board and lace it tightly across the back using quilting thread.

Because embroidery is a tactile medium and many of the stitches are dimensional, do not use glass to cover the framed embroidery unless the piece will be displayed in a particularly dusty area. When using glass with embroidery, ensure that it is raised away from the stitching by placing spacers between the embroidery and the glass. Mat board is one material that can be used for these spacers. Whenever necessary, the embroidery can be unlaced and washed.

CHRISTMAS CARDINALS, A MOUNTED AND FRAMED CREWEL EMBROIDERY BY AUTHOR JUDY JEROY.

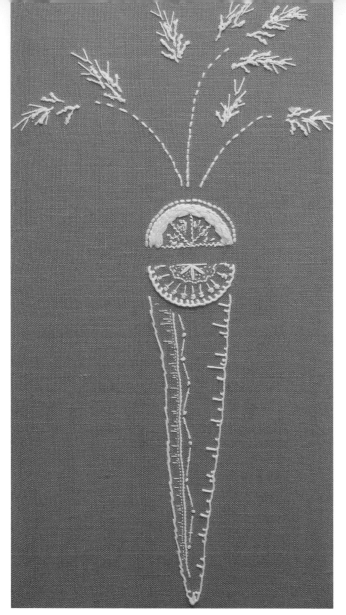

SUSAN DAWSON'S *TURQUOISE CARROT*

S T I T C H E S

There is no difference between crewel embroidery stitches and regular embroidery stitches. A stitch learned in crewel embroidery can be employed in any other embroidery technique. In some shapes and motifs, such as satin and long and short shading, for example, it is helpful to draw light guidelines on the fabric using a hard lead pencil.

Flat
STITCHES

❈

Flat stitches lie flat on the surface of the material, either closely together or at regularly spaced intervals. The stitches can be crossed or not. The base stitches may be raised off the fabric on bars, or they can be whipped or threaded with other threads. Flat stitches are more light reflective, and when worked with a smooth thread such as silk or cotton, they can be very shiny. Worked with wool or some other fuzzy thread, flat stitches cover the ground area more easily. Long and short shading is easily worked in crewel wool because the hairs of the thread blend with each other, making the shading more subtle.

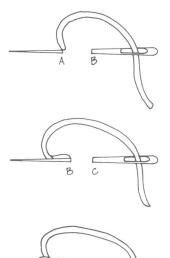

OUTLINE

Working left to right with the needle held directly on the line, bring the needle up at A, yarn up, needle down at B and up again at A. Pull through, yarn up over the needle. Down at C and up at B. Continue, keeping the yarn over the needle.

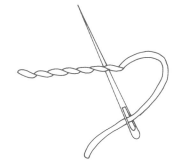

WHIPPED OUTLINE

Slip the needle under the first half of one stitch and the second half of another. The needle whips from the side opposite that on which the yarn was held. Note the slant of the needle. Do not pierce the fabric. Tug gently after every three or four stitches to tighten.

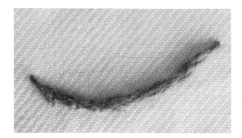

Stem (or Crewel)

Follow the directions for the outline stitch, but hold the yarn below the line instead of above. This results in a more textured or corded line.

WHIPPED STEM

Follow the directions for whipped outline, but slant the needle from the opposite side. Do not pierce the fabric. Tug gently after every three or four stitches to tighten.

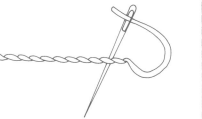
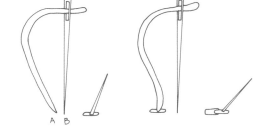

SPLIT STITCH

Bring needle up at A and down at B, taking a very small, short stitch.

Work the next and each succeeding stitch by bringing up the needle through the previous stitch, splitting the thread. Take the thread down a very short distance away.

Continue in this manner, stitching a fine, tight line.

RAISED OUTLINE

Lay bars to fit the shape.

Bring the needle up at A. Slide the needle under the first bar. Proceed to work the stitch as ordinary outline, but pick up a bar each time instead of a bit of fabric. Snug up each stitch by pulling upward. At the end of each row, sink the needle and begin next row at same point as previous row.

Pack the stitches slightly with a fingernail for better coverage.

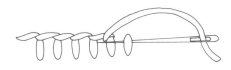

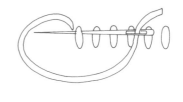

RAISED STEM

Work as for raised outline, but work the stitch as ordinary stem with the thread below the needle.

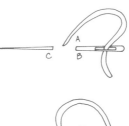

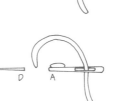

BACKSTITCH

Bring the needle up at A, down at B, and up again at C, then down again at A and up at D, working right to left. Each stitch shares a hole with the previous stitch.

WHIPPED BACKSTITCH

After stitching a row of backstitch, slip the needle under each stitch, not piercing the fabric. Pull up after every three or four stitches to tighten. Note that the needle whips from one side only.

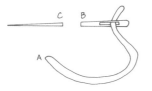

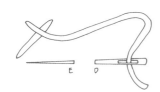

HERRINGBONE OR LADDER STITCH

Bring the needle up at A on the bottom line, then down at B and up at C, both on upper line.

Making a diagonal stitch, insert the needle at D and up at E on the bottom line.

Move again to the top line and repeat the process. Remember, when the needle is above, the thread is below; when the needle is below, the thread is above.

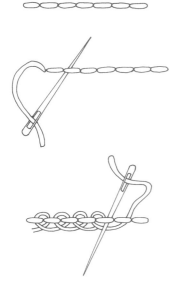

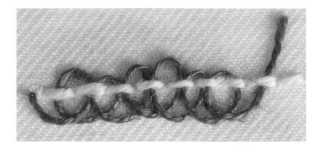

PEKINESE

Lay a row of backstitches. Lace or whip in each stitch with a contrasting thread.

Note that needle is inserted up behind one backstitch and then down behind the preceding backstitch. Keep the tension even, and a bit loose.

RUNNING STITCH

Bring the thread up at A. Insert the needle at B, up at C, in at D, and up at E. Pull the thread through. Try to keep the stitches about twice as long as the spaces between.

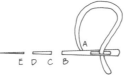

THREADED RUNNING STITCH

Work two evenly spaced rows of running stitches. Weave a second thread through the stitches as shown, taking care not to pierce the fabric.

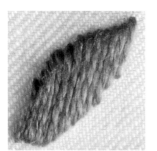

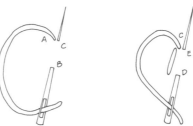

SATIN AND SLANTED SATIN

Bring the thread up at A, down at B, and up at C—which is slightly farther away than right next to A. Insert the needle at D and up at E; this keeps the stitches at a nice angle. The yarn is carried across the back. Emphasize the slant.

Notice the direction of stitches and the change made when moving along a curved space. Achieve this through the use of wedge stitches, indicated by the arrows. Keep the edges as even as possible; the use of split stitch outline may help.

WEAVING OR DARNING STITCH

Begin the pattern so that first line of stitching runs through the widest part of area to be covered.

Pick up one or two threads of fabric at regularly spaced intervals. At the end of one run of stitches, reverse the needle direction and run a parallel line of stitches a thread or two away. Alternate the threads picked up to achieve an interesting pattern. This stitch is easier to work on an even-weave fabric where the threads can be counted.

SEED STITCH

Take small single stitches in various directions at random to establish an irregular pattern of dots. For a very pronounced pattern, work the stitches in pairs or re-work each stitch to double it.

BURDEN STITCH

The long laid threads show up as tiny glimpses of color between the satin stitches. In the drawing, note the use of half-size compensating stitches at the edges. Shading is easy with this stitch.

Lay long threads, or bars, across the width of the work. Work spaced satin stitch over the bars, leaving room between stitches for another stitch. Work the next row in a bricking pattern across the next laid thread and between the stitches in the first row.

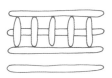
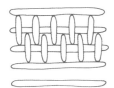

NEW ENGLAND LAID
OR
ROMANIAN STITCH

This stitch is also called "economy stitch" because very little thread is used on the back of the fabric.

Working from left to right, or from top to bottom, bring the needle up at A, down at B, and up at C. Next, the thread crosses original stitch and goes down at D and up at E. Repeat the sequence B to C, then D to E.

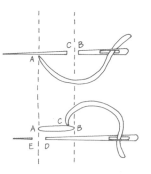

FLAT STITCH

This stitch is also called the Economy Stitch because the yarn doesn't carry across on the back side.

Working from left to right, bring the needle up at A, down at B, and up at C.

Reverse the needle and go down at D and up at E. Repeat the sequence, B to C, D to E.

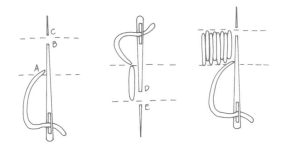

LONG AND SHORT SHADING

The principle of long and short shading is to provide a smooth blend of color, filling the shape or motif in a natural flow. The technique is achieved by the use of satin stitches, worked in irregular lengths for the first row. Succeeding rows are satin stitches worked into the previous row in such a manner as to provide a smooth transition of color. The wool shades that are used must be chosen carefully; distinct steps will be visible if the shades are too far apart.

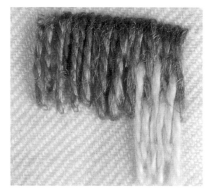

Shapes and motifs may have as few as two values of one color or as many other values or colors as desired to achieve the preferred result. Shading may be light edges to dark centers or the reverse. A light source should be considered when planning the design; that is, determine the direction from which the sun shines on the flower or leaf and make that edge lighter in color than the shadowed area.

It is desirable to achieve a clear, crisp edge that covers the transfer line completely. Three different edges can be used: buttonhole long and short, long and short over a split stitch outline of the shape, or simply long and short following the outline.

Consider the direction that you intend the eye to follow. For instance, in a flower shape, aim toward the flower center by holding the working thread in the direction of the center and taking the thread down at that point. It may be necessary to skip a few stitches in order not to pack the threads too closely. Just be sure the fabric is covered. If the worked area becomes too hairy, check to ensure the wool is threaded with the nap the correct way.

Only for the first row are both long and short stitches used. For subsequent rows in the shaded shape, just long stitches will be used.

Use a hard lead pencil to divide the shape with a number of horizontal curved lines to define the color divisions. Draw vertical guidelines slanting toward the center of the shape.

Start the first row at the center of the top. Place a long stitch that extends across the marked line and halfway into the next section. The next stitch should be immediately beside the first and should extend just to the line. Continue alternating a long stitch with a short stitch, slanting as you progress around the curve, keeping to the vertical guidelines. When one side of the shape has been stitched, finish the other side, beginning at the middle again and working to the edge.

Buttonhole Edge Long and Short Shading is used when a definite corded edge is desired to distinguish the petals from each other. All other directions for long and short shading remain the same.

Begin the stitching at the rightmost point of the shape with two or three tiny buttonhole stitches. Then take a long buttonhole stitch, placing it so the thread covers the straight ends of the previous stitches and establishes the correct slant. Proceed around the shape, alternating long and short stitches, following the guide lines for stitch direction.

Completing the Shape

The second step is the same, regardless which stitch was used to outline the shape. Use the next-to-lightest value if you've begun with the lightest value.

As you stitch, come up from the back of the fabric and split into the threads of the first row at as shallow an angle as possible. Working up into the previous stitches this way creates the least possible disruption of the original row, with no pulls or holes. Take the thread down into an unworked area, being careful to keep the slant correct. Using the horizontal guide lines, place staggered long stitches across the shape.

Continue to repeat this second step with the remaining color values until the darkest is used for only a few stitches at the base of the motif. At this time some short stitches will be necessary to finish the base.

Chained
STITCHES

✣

This family of stitches carries the loop stitch a step further. After bending the thread into a loop, the needle is inserted into the same hole. The loop is held into a chain link with an additional link or with a tack stitch. When worked with a thin thread, tiny stitches, and tight tension, very little or none of the fabric shows through the links of the chain. An entirely different effect is achieved when a heavy thread is stitched loosely, allowing the fabric to show through.

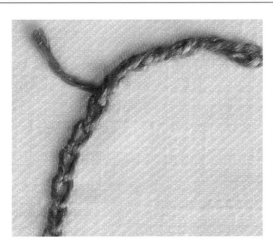

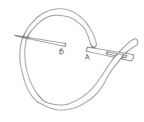

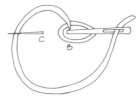

CHAIN STITCH

Bring the needle up at A; pull through. Make a loop up and around to the left, holding the thread with the left thumb. Insert the needle at A and bring out at B. Pull the needle through the loop and down toward you. Do not pull the loop up too tightly.

Repeat the step above, inserting the needle at B, inside first loop and in the same hole. Bring the needle up at C and pull through. Continue in this manner. When the line is complete, make a tack stitch to hold the last loop in place.

WHIPPED CHAIN

Bring the needle to the surface close to the tack-down and slip it under both loops of the last chain. Do not pierce the fabric. Continue under both loops of each chain, whipping from one side only. Pull up firmly after every three or four stitches to tighten.

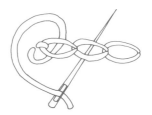

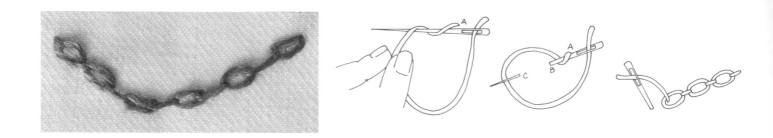

CABLE CHAIN

Bring the thread up at A. Hold the needle in your right hand, grasping the thread in your left. Wrap the thread once around the needle as shown.

Still holding the thread in your left hand, snug it around the needle. Insert the point at B, bring it out at C, and bring the thread under the point of the needle. Pull it snug. Pull the needle and thread through.

Continue to the end of the line. End the stitch by making a long tack stitch, pulling the thread to the back. Make the spaces between C and B a little longer than the spaces between B and A.

HEAVY CHAIN BRAID

Thread three or more contrasting colors through a large needle. Begin the stitch as for regular chain (page 000), but make a very long tack stitch.

Bring the needle up at A and slip it through tack stitch. Go down again at A and pull through. Come up at B and slip through the original chain. Continue in this manner, sliding the next stitch through the one two loops back, producing a heavy chain braid.

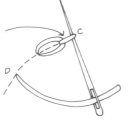

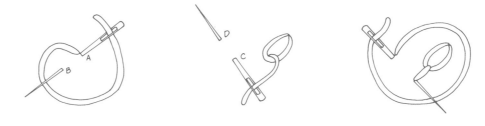

CHAINED FEATHER

Bring the thread up at A and down at A, then up at B, looping the thread under the needle. Insert the needle at C and out at D; pull it through. This completes a detached chain. Loop down and around on a diagonal. The needle is in again at D and up at C with a loop under the needle. Insert the needle at E and up at F; pull it through. This creates a series of detached chains at angles to each other with the appearance of feather stitch.

DETACHED CHAIN (LAZY DAISY)

Bring the thread up at A and pull through. Make a loop in the direction of the other end of the petal. Insert the needle in the same hole as A, bring up at B and pull the thread up through the loop, pulling in the direction the needle points, until a loose loop is formed. Insert the needle in the fabric on the outside of the loop to form a tack stitch.

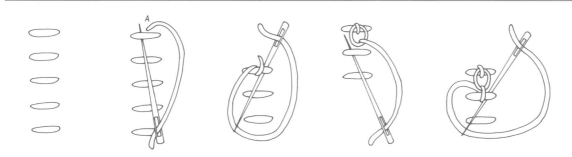

RAISED CHAIN ON A BAR

Lay bars to fill the desired shape. These are the only parts of the stitch to show on the back. Bring the needle up at A and slide it under first bar, slanting from the bar to slightly left of center at the top of the same bar. Do not pierce the fabric.

Pull up carefully. Loop the yarn down and to the right. Slip the needle under the same bar, top to bottom, just to the right of A. Pull through the loop carefully and repeat.

Continue to the bottom, taking the needle down at bottom center of the shape. End and begin each new row at the top.

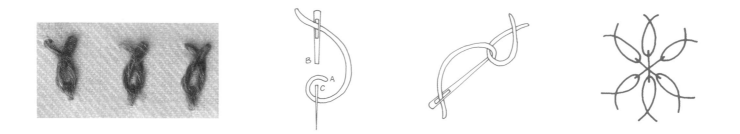

DETACHED TWISTED CHAIN

Bring the thread up at A and make a loop. Insert the needle at B and bring out at C, making a slanting stitch back to the line. Pull through gently, forming a detached chain. Tack down as shown.

To create a floret shape, space twisted chains in a circle with all the tack-down stitches in the same central hole as shown.

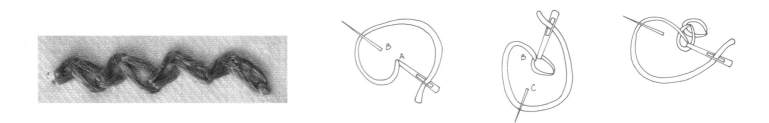

ZIGZAG CHAIN

Bring the thread up at A. Make a loop up and around and hold it in place with your thumb. Insert the needle again at A, bring it up at B, slanting the stitch diagonally across the line. The loop formed should be longer than for a regular chain stitch. Pull the thread up through the loop.

Next make a loop down and around at a diagonal; hold it in place with your thumb. Insert the needle in the same hole B and bring up at C. Pull the thread up. Continue zigzagging back and forth at right angles. Be careful to have at least a right angle and no less or the stitch will fall on itself and look sloppy.

Knotted
STITCHES

❈

Knotted stitches are made by twisting the thread around the needle before the needle is reinserted into the fabric. Many of the knot stitches can be used separately, scattered to fill an area. Because of the textural character of knot stitches, they can add variety to the other families of stitches. Please note that French knot and bullion stitches have a "grain" or directional quality, depending on whether the needle is inserted at the north, south, east, or west point of the thread emerging from the fabric. Very little light reflection occurs with knotted stitches, which often makes the thread color appear darker than in the flat stitches.

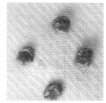

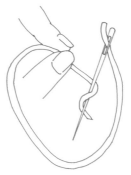

FRENCH KNOT

Hold the thread with thumb and forefinger about 2 inches (5 cm) from the point where the thread emerged from the fabric.

Wind the needle once around the thread in a clockwise motion.

Lock the thread under the point of the needle with the knot formed close to the fabric.

Insert the point of the needle a scant few threads from where thread came up—almost in the same place. Pull to the back to lock.

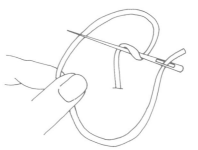

LONG ARM FRENCH KNOT

Work as for a French knot up to the last step. Insert the point of the needle a distance away from where thread came up, forming a tail.

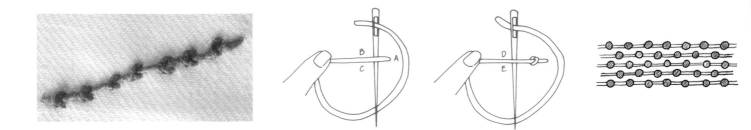

CORAL KNOT

Working right to left, bring the needle up at A on the working line. Lay the yarn to the left and hold it under the thumb. Insert the needle at B and bring it up at C, making a small stitch under the line. Loop the thread under the needle, making a knot when pulled up. Repeat with the needle down at D and up at E. Knots should be spaced so that a knot would just fit between them.

When working coral knots in rows, as in shading, the knots should be spaced so that in the row below, the knots will fit between those above (bricking). Work rows from the same end so that the needle will be pointed toward unworked areas and all knots will be in the same direction.

BULLION KNOT

The use of a long, very narrow needle, such as a beading or milliner's needle, may make the bullion knots easier to work.

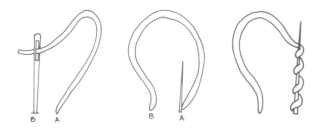

Bring the needle up at A and down at B, leaving a loop of yarn on top.

Bring the needle halfway up at A again.

Take the yarn as it comes from A, wind it around needle enough times so that the coil will cover the distance from A to B. Do not stretch the yarn.

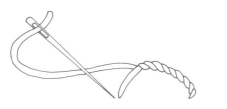

Grasp the coil of yarn between left thumb and forefinger, hold the needle under the fabric, and move the needle up and down slightly until it moves freely. Still holding the coil with left hand, grasp the point of the needle, and work needle through the coil of yarn. Pull all the way through, drawing the yarn in direction in which knot will lie (toward point B). Tug gently on the yarn, pushing the coil back toward A with point of needle until the knot is smooth. Needle down at the end of the knot.

BULLION ROSETTES

To make rosettes, work three bullion knots to form a triangle. Then work one bullion knot to wrap around one corner of the triangle, putting a few extra twists on the needle so that the knot curls around instead of lying straight. Next add another bullion knot, overlapping half the previous one.

Work around the triangle in this way until the rose is formed.

RAISED CUP STITCH

Work a triangle of backstitches. Bring the thread up at a corner; slip the needle under one backstitch. With the thread over and then under the needle, draw up knot. Continue making two knots on each backstitch. On the next row, work two knots between each two knots of the first row. Work around and around until the cup is the desired size. Finish off by piercing the worked cup and ending on the back.

TRELLIS STITCH

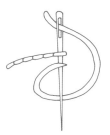

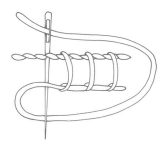

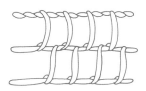

Work a row of back stitches around the shape. Come up slightly below a back stitch, inside the circle (X). Slide the needle under the back stitch and place the thread first over, then under, the knot. Continue this stitch until you are back at the first stitch, then work the stitch into the first row of stitches instead of into the back stitches. As the circle is worked, decrease the number of stitches by skipping a stitch now and then.

End off by pulling last few stitches tight, and either sink into the fabric or work through stitches back to the row of back stitches and then down. The shape can be stuffed with similar thread, cotton balls, felt, or a stone or jewel.

LOOPED
STITCHES

✤

These stitches are formed by bending or curving the thread into a loop and then holding the curve with another stitch. The angles formed by the following stitches vary, but the concept of the stitch is the same. The stitches may be worked closely together or with fabric showing.

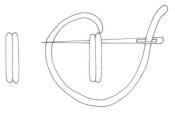

DETACHED BUTTONHOLE BARS

Lay two strands of wool (only one for non-stretchy yarn), sharing the same holes. Bring the needle up at the top and work buttonhole stitch around the two-strand bar. Keeping an even tension, work buttonhole stitches along length of bar. When the bar is filled, take the needle down just outside the edge of the bar at left. Allow the bar to roll and twist on itself.

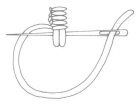

DETACHED BUTTONHOLE ARC

Work as for a bar to the halfway point. Stretch to create a curved shape and tack it in place by catching a few threads of fabric as you make the next stitch. Continue detached stitches to end, tacking as necessary to maintain the shape.

DETACHED BUTTONHOLE CIRCLES

Visually divide the circle into three triangles. Work a detached buttonhole arc in each triangle so that together they fill the circle. Tack as necessary to maintain equal curves around the circle. Continue from one arc to the next, taking care to maintain the stitching rhythm.

OPEN BUTTONHOLE OR BLANKET STITCH

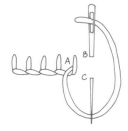

To eliminate the hook created by the beginning of the buttonhole stitch itself, work a straight stitch from the top of the line to A. Bring the thread up in same hole as A. Make a loop to the bottom of the line and hold with the thumb. Insert the needle at B and bring it out at C, with the thread beneath the needle. Repeat the B to C part of the stitch.

CLOSE BUTTONHOLE

Work left to right, with the needle pointing toward your left arm (if you are right-handed). Work a straight stitch across the stitching area to eliminate the hook at the beginning of the buttonhole stitch itself. Bring the needle up at A. Insert the needle at B, right beside the straight stitch, and up at C with the yarn looped down under the needle. Repeat this step being careful to completely cover the fabric while not crowding the stitches. The looped edges of the stitch should form an even row of little "pearls."

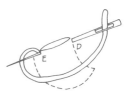

Buttonhole wheels can be worked to fill a circle or just to decorate the perimeter.

INNER BUTTONHOLE WHEEL

Bring the needle up at the edge of the circle. Insert the needle in the center of the circle and bring it up at the edge, catching the buttonhole loop. Space the stitching evenly around the circle. Loop the last stitch under first stitch to achieve a smooth buttonhole loop.

OUTER BUTTONHOLE WHEEL

Bring the needle up at the edge of the circle. Insert the needle outside the circle, a short distance from the edge, and bring it up again at the circle edge, catching the buttonhole loop. Space the stitches evenly. Loop the last stitch under first stitch to achieve a smooth buttonhole loop.

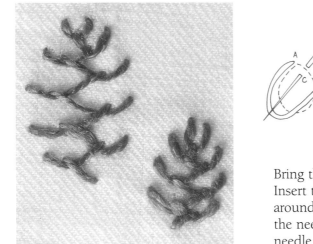

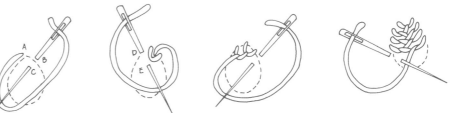

CRETAN STITCH

Bring the thread up at A. Make a loop down and around to the right. Insert the needle at B and bring it out at C. Loop the thread down and around to the left. Insert the needle at D, and up at E. Continue swinging the needle to the right and to the left, looping the thread. The angle of the needle flattens as the shape is filled.

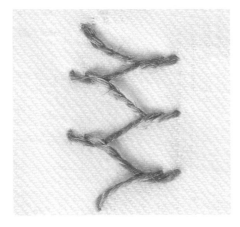

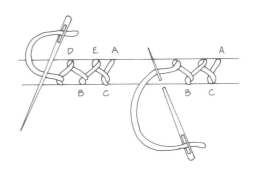

FAGOTING STITCH

Bring the thread up at A. Make a loop down and around to the right. Insert the needle at B and bring it out at C. Loop thread down and around to the left. Insert the needle at D and up at E. Continue swinging the needle to the right and to the left, looping the thread. The angle of the needle flattens as the shape is filled.

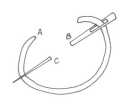

FEATHER STITCH

Bring the thread up at A, making a loop down and under the needle; then down at B and up at C.

Swing the needle to the other side of the shape to be followed. Insert at D and up at E with the thread looped under the needle. Continue in this manner, swinging the needle back and forth.

HALF FEATHER STITCH

Half feather is worked like feather stitch, but the needle is inserted on one side only.

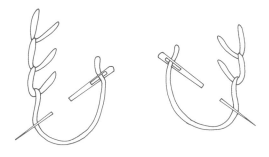

FISHBONE

Bring the needle up at A and down at B, making this stitch long enough to set the slant for subsequent stitches, at least ⅓ the length of the shape to be stitched if the shape is less than 1½ inches (3.75 cm) long. Bring the needle up at C and down at D, crossing over the first stitch; then needle up at E and down at F, crossing the first two stitches. Continue alternating sides. The last two stitches should meet at the same hole.

SERRATED FISHBONE

This stitch is worked like the fishbone stitch, but with a staggered edge. Just make alternating stitches slightly longer.

FLY

Bring the needle up at A, loop the yarn as if making a chain stitch, and down at B. Bring the needle up at C and down at D to tack the loop.

Many variations of the fly stitch can be achieved by changing the length of tack-down stitch and/or adjusting placement of the "arms."

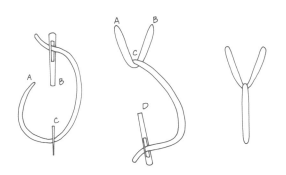

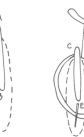
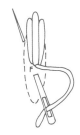

CLOSED FLY

Bring the needle up at A, slightly beyond the tip of the stitching area, and down at B. This stitch should be ⅓ to ½ the length if the shape to be stitched is less than 1½ inches (3.75 cm). Bring the needle up at C, loop the yarn as if making a chain stitch, go down at D and up at E. Tack the loop at F.

Continue placing stitches next to each other so that no fabric shows between them. Maintain a proper slant to the stitches.

Needlelace and Weaving

❋

Needlelace stitches can be worked over a series of spokes or bars in the entirety, or they can be worked detached from the fabric except for the beginning and ending. They can be linked or knotted or whipped, depending on the individual stitch. Thicker threads—which are difficult to stitch through fabric—may be used on raised spokes or bars since they will only pierce the fabric at the beginning and the end of the stitch.

Spider Web stitches are all worked over spokes or bars which pierce the fabric. In most cases, the spokes/bars are filled from the smallest area to the largest, or from the center to the outer edges. In all cases, the spokes should extend at least two thread widths beyond the perimeter of the circle so the finished work will adequately cover the shape. Dramatic color changes can be very effective in this type of stitch.

WHIPPED SPIDER

Working from right to left, go backward over one spoke and forward under two spokes, snugging up the thread each time. Work around somewhat tightly to make the ribs, or whips, stand out.

There are many effective treatments and shapes of spider webs. One variation is to whip only part of each spoke, leaving the outer portion unworked.

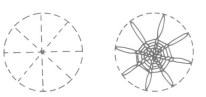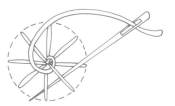

RING SPIDER

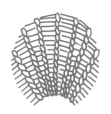

For this variation, work the spokes as straight stitches without filling the center of the ring. Work in a circle, filling the shape.

CRESCENT OR FAN SPIDER

This version is worked the same way as the other whipped spiders, except that the yarn must be carried on the back of the work so it will be in position to start at the beginning of each row.

HORIZONTAL SPIDER

This is an effective stitch for leaves. The center line (indicated by arrows) is worked first. Then work the rest, alternating between the sides, filling back and forth, sinking the needle at the ends.

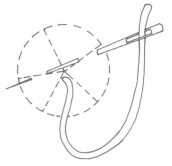

WOVEN SPIDER

Lay an uneven number of spokes, all stitches coming up at the outer edge of the circle and going down at the center. Bring the needle up in the middle slightly off center and between two spokes. Weave under and over the spokes, round and round, until the shape is filled. Sink the thread immediately under a spoke.

CEYLON STITCH

Several rows of this stitch worked together give the appearance of knitting. There will be long carryovers on the back.

Make one row of detached open buttonhole stitches (page 41), catching the fabric with only the upper edges of the stitches. Work the next row from left to right again, but this time catch the base of each stitch of the row above. The needle does not pierce the fabric except at each side.

INTERLACED BUTTONHOLE

Stitch warp threads ¼ inch (.5 cm) apart, or closer if yarn is lighter in weight than veloura. Come up at the side. Buttonhole over the top warp and then over the second warp; repeat across the row. For the next row, use the second and third warps, fitting stitches between the previous stitches. Fill densely.

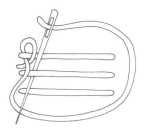

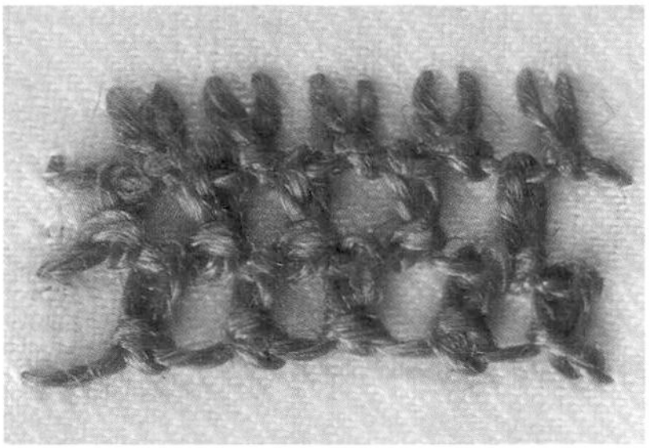

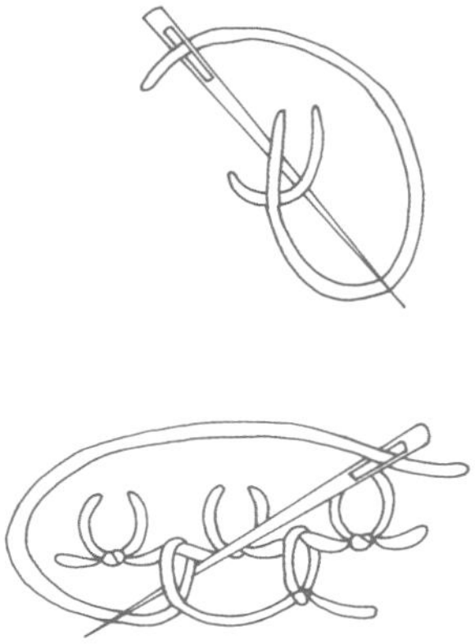

Knotted Buttonhole Filling

The stitch may be worked as shown, piercing the fabric at top and edges, or it can be worked over a foundation of back stitches. After making the open buttonhole stitch, slide the needle under both threads of the first loop and over the working thread to form a knot. Work back and forth.

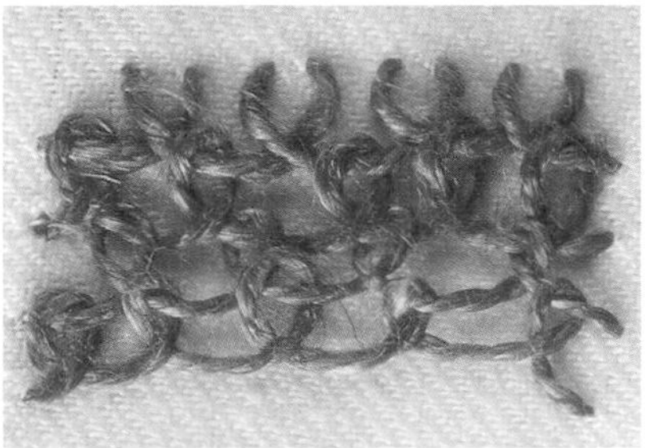

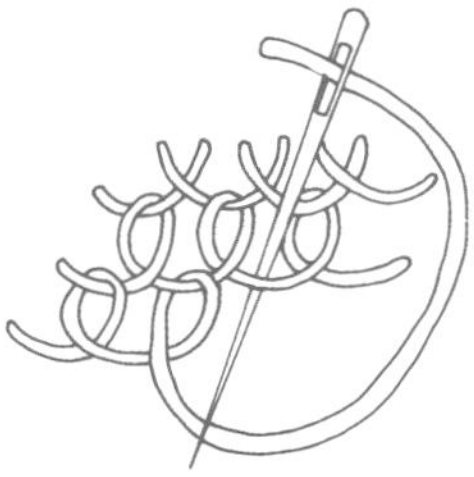

Open Buttonhole Filling

This is a detached stitch which can be used either to hold a gem or stone or as a lacy covering. Only the edge stitches penetrate the fabric; do not pierce the fabric when working the filling. The stitches are worked from left to right and back again.

COUCHED and LAID STITCHES

For these stitches, the yarn lies on top of the fabric with very little on the back and is tacked down by small holding stitches. Because of this manner of stitching, very little thread is wasted on the back. Beautiful ornamental fillings can be achieved with this method.

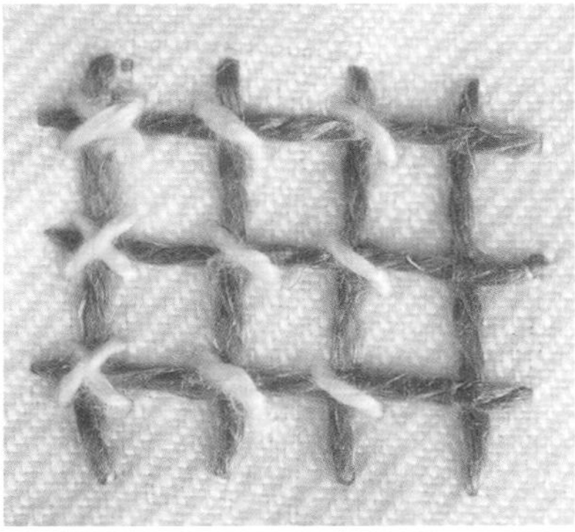

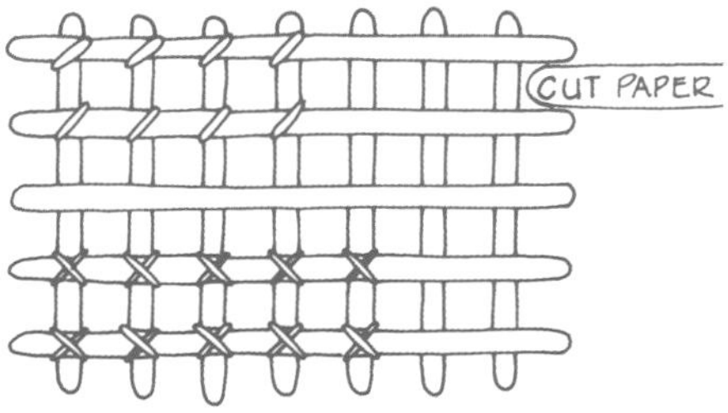

Simple Filling

To lay consistent lines, cut an index card cut to the desired width as shown. Lay all the lines in one direction, then lay the perpendicular threads so that the spaces formed are absolutely square. Tack down the crossed threads at each intersection.

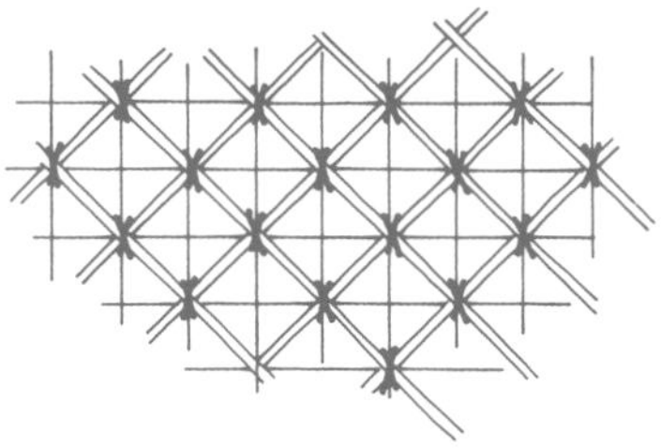

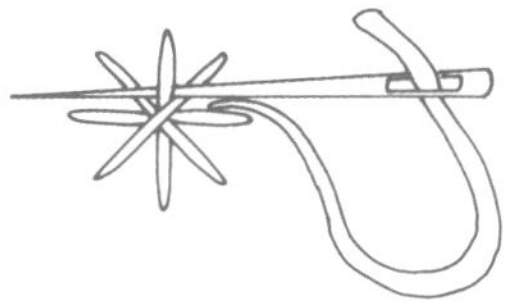

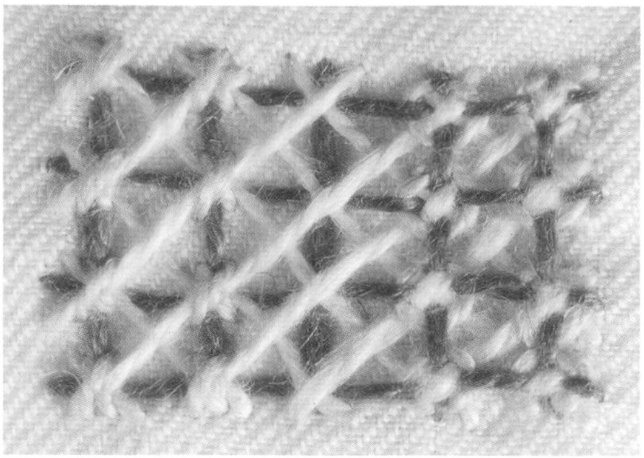

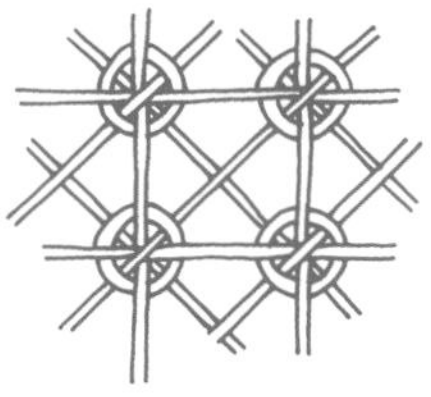

Double Filling

Lay simple filling as above, but without tacking down the crossed threads. Spaces must be perfect squares for second layer to work correctly. With a contrasting thread, place another layer of lines crossing every intersection of the first filling and forming crosses in spaces left by the first layer.

With a third thread color, tack down all four threads—the two from the first layer and two from second—at the intersections where all four meet. Use either one stitch or a cross stitch as tack-downs. The drawing shows an enlargement of the tack-down stitches.

Fancy Overlaid Filler

The tack-down is woven around the four layers of thread as shown, picking up the bottom layers and going over the top layers. Sink the thread just beyond the point where it came up.

DIMENSIONAL STITCHES

Members of this group of stitches are three-dimensional. In effect, they stand away from the fabric. They can be formed over wire, on paper (which is then torn away) or on fabric (which is cut away).

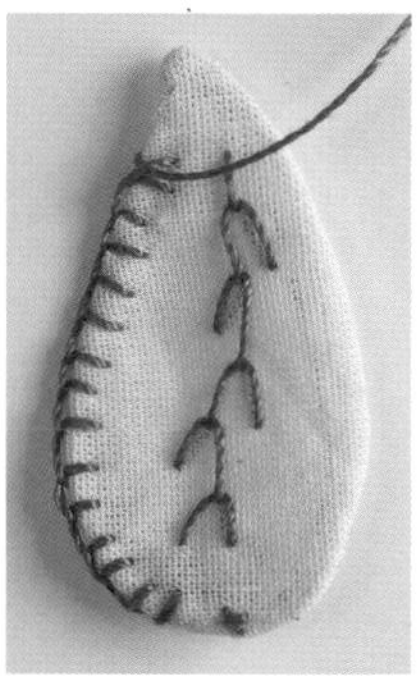

Detached Butterfly Wing Over Wire

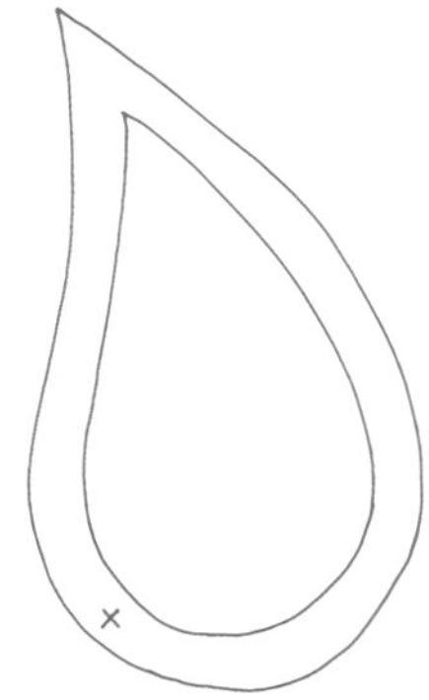

Gauge 20-30 floral wire works best for this stitch design.

Cut a wing shape from fabric, allowing ¼ inch (.5 cm) seam allowance around the outer edge. Fold under and finger press the seam allowance. Unfold, and work a row of running stitches just outside the fold line with basting thread. The X indicates the point at which the wing will attach to the embroidered butterfly.

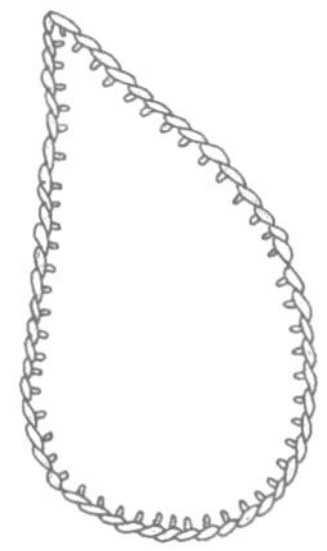

Form 20- or 30-gauge floral wire to the appropriate wing shape. Hold the wire against the back of the wing fabric and draw up the stitching to hold the wire in place. Work buttonhole stitch (page 35) closely around folded shape, securing the wire within the fold.

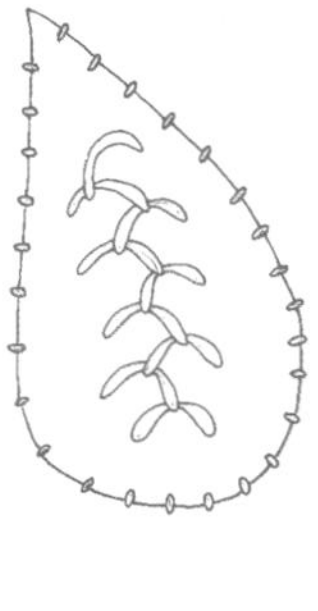

Using the same thread as for the buttonhole stitch, work an open row of alternating feather stitch (page 37). To attach the wing to the background fabric, take a few stitches with the same thread.

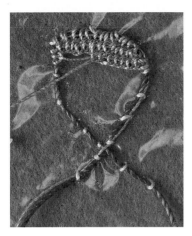

DETACHED BUTTONHOLE PETAL ON FABRIC

Using a very firm, heavy fabric inserted into a plastic bag, place a petal pattern drawn on paper inside the plastic bag, making a sandwich of all materials. Lay a piece of ribbon or heavy thread along the pattern line and sew through all layers of the sandwich with a disposable thin thread, couching around the heavy thread/ribbon.

With the line couched down, work the buttonhole filling as described. When the filling is complete, snip the thin, disposable thread and pull it out from the back to release the petal shape.

With ribbon for the couched line and sewing thread in the needle, couch an outline around each petal, beginning and ending at the base of petal. Leave a 3-inch (7.5 cm) waste tail to begin and end each thread. The spacing of the couching threads can be used to advantage if it is kept consistent.

Use a different thread, such as pearl cotton, as the working thread. Attach it by sliding up under couched threads, up the left side and across the top. This thread will then be carried back to the left as the first "return warp."

Begin working detached buttonhole stitch, catching in the couched line at the top and also in the return warp. The buttonhole loops never pierce the base fabric.

Work to fill the shape, increasing and decreasing on the sides as is necessary. Don't make the loops too tight as this will cause distortion. All rows should lie flat. On the last row, catch up the loops of the previous row, the return warp, and the couched line at the base of the petal. On the back, carefully cut the sewing thread used to couch the line.

(This causes the worked shape to detach from the holding fabric.) The waste tails will be used to secure the petal. Work the other embroidery on the flower before attaching the petals to the main embroidery.

DETACHED BUTTONHOLE RING

Wind a 20 inch (50 cm) length of thread around a finger two or three times, catching tail within the winding. Work buttonhole stitch over the thread completely around the ring. Join the last stitch to the first. Remove from finger and push the ring into a bow shape. Attach to fabric with end thread.

A detached buttonhole ring also can be worked using a bone or plastic ring instead of a finger.

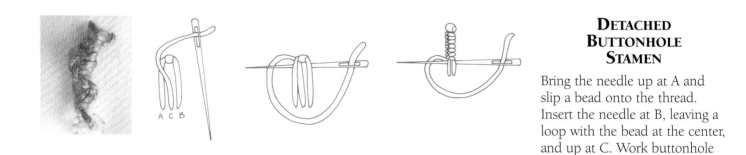

DETACHED BUTTONHOLE STAMEN

Bring the needle up at A and slip a bead onto the thread. Insert the needle at B, leaving a loop with the bead at the center, and up at C. Work buttonhole stitch, over all three threads, from the bead down to the fabric. Take the thread down to back of the fabric and secure it.

DETACHED CRETAN PETAL
ON PAPER

Draw the shape of the petal on a sheet of notebook paper. Crumple the paper in your hand to soften and strengthen it, then place it in an embroidery hoop. Using an away waste knot (x) and one strand of a hard thread such as rayon, cotton or linen, work a row of chain stitch around the entire outer edge of the petal. Then work down the middle vein. Thread the long end of the working thread through stitches on the back of paper to the base of petal where you began.

With a full, long strand of thread in a contrasting color value, and an away waste knot, work loose cretan stitch down one side of the petal, using the inside bar of the outer chain and the center vein chain. Slide the needle through to get into position to work cretan down the remaining side of the petal. Work the same on the other side of the petal, back to the beginning.

Pull the end of the working thread out at the end beside the chain thread. Tear away the paper from around the outer edges of the petal, then lift the remainder of the paper carefully from the inside areas. Use the long thread ends to fasten the petal to the background fabric.

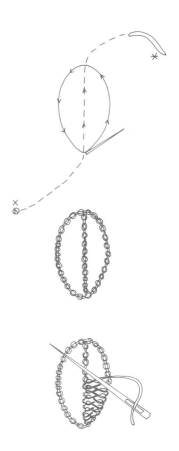

RAISED CLOSE HERRINGBONE

Place a tack stitch from A to B at the top of the shape to be filled.

Bring the needle out at the base of the shape (C) and slide it under the tack stitch. Put the needle through fabric at D and out at E, which is slightly above D. Slide the needle under the tack stitch again. Continue stitching through the fabric, a little higher up each time, and sliding under the tack. Allow the thread to build up to create a padded shape.

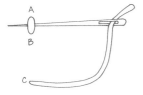  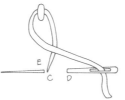 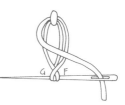

P R O J E C T S

Here are a few projects to help you practice the stitches and perhaps to stretch your skills into new areas. It might be a good idea to first try the stitches on a scrap piece of fabric ("doodle cloth") to iron out any difficulties with a particular stitch. If you aren't pleased with the appearance of a stitch, keep working at it. Once your stitch quality improves, then you can stitch it on your project.

The projects that follow are categorized by level of difficulty. There are six projects for beginners. A beginner is one who has never tried stitching surface embroidery with a sharp needle. There are two projects at the intermediate skill level. An intermediate stitcher is one who is familiar with crewel stitches and a sharp needle. Finally, there are two more challenging projects that involve three-dimensional techniques.

EARLY AMERICAN ROSE

PATTERN ON PAGE 69

Skill level: Beginner

Authentic colors and stitches are used in this reproduction of a rose done in Early American times. The stitches used are ladder, buttonhole wheels and spokes, weaving, seed, flat, and New England laid stitch. Historically, there was a rationale behind the use of these particular stitches: wool was scarce and economy was the order of the day, so very little thread was wasted on the backside of the design. The colors used are those which could have been reproduced by the colonists from dyes derived from indigo, cochineal, mayweed, woad, cocklebur, sumac, pokeberry, and fustic. Choose a plain weave linen fabric similar to that available at the time.

MATERIALS

DMC Medici crewel wool: blue 8208; green 8407, 8408, and 8411; rose 8101, 8816, and 8817.

DMC 6-strand cotton: yellow #727

Plain weave linen: 15 x 15 inches (38 x 38 cm)

Chenille needles: two #24

INSTRUCTIONS

Transfer the design to the plain weave linen using graphite carbon transfer paper. Use a screw-adjustable hoop for all stitches except line stitches, such as stem, outline, and chain, which may be worked soft in the hand.

All of the major stem is worked in whipped chain using a medium green wool. Smaller stems are worked in whipped outline or whipped stem in light green wool.

Work the main rose in three values of rose wool, lightest on the outer petals, and medium and dark rose in the middle using Rumanian couching/New England laid stitch. Notice that only a small bite of the fabric is taken, leaving very little wool on the back side of the fabric. The center of the flower is worked in buttonhole wheel with two pieces of yellow 6-strand cotton. The outer leaves are stitched with yellow green wool in New England laid stitch.

The smaller flower is worked the same as the main one with the three values of rose wool. Work the underneath leaves in fly stitch using the light green wool.

The two leaves below the rose have a darning pattern in light green wool in the outer portions of the leaves. This is an over-under (running stitch) type of pattern; you can skip a row of threads between each line of stitches or not. It might help to work out the pattern first on paper to determine if you will stitch over three threads and under one thread or some other pattern. The center of the leaves is worked in ladder (herringbone) stitch in dark green wool. After all stitching is done, work outline stitch in dark green wool around the entire shape to define the lines.

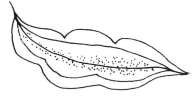

There are two sprigs of tiny blue buds, one at the top left and the other at the bottom right. The flower buds are stitched in blue wool in either outer buttonhole wheel with a void in the center or inner buttonhole wheel. Refer to photo for placement.

The large leaf at the bottom of the piece is worked in dark green wool in flat stitch. After stitching both sides of the leaf, define the edges with a row of outline stitch in dark green wool. There is a center line down the void in outline stitch in light green wool. Seed stitch is used scattered within the void in blue wool.

"STITCH A MEMORY"

PATTERN ON PAGE 70

A whimsical bird sitting within a heart of white lace is surrounded by polychrome flowers.
This delicate design deserves a special place in your heart and in your home.

MATERIALS

Appleton crewel wools: rose #s 752, 754, 755, and 756; green #s 335, 541, 543, and 544; blue #s 741, 742, 744, and 745; yellow #s 472, 474, and 841

DMC Medici crewel wool: white

DMC 6-strand cotton: yellow

DMC #8 pearl cotton: white

Natural linen twill: 15 x 15 inches (38 x 38 cm)

Chenille Needles: two #24

INSTRUCTIONS

Transfer the designs to the linen twill using graphite carbon transfer paper. Use a screw-adjustable hoop for all stitches except line stitches, such as stem, outline, and chain, which may be worked soft in the hand.

All of the major branch is worked in chain using a medium olive green wool. Smaller stems are worked in whipped outline or whipped stem in light to medium green wool.

The white lace frame around the heart consists of two rows of feather stitch with pekinese stitch worked between them. The feather stitch nearest the heart is white Medici wool in a variation pattern that consists of three stitches each way (see photograph). The pekinese stitch has the backstitches worked in white pearl cotton and then laced with white Medici wool; take care to keep backstitch and lacing even. The outer border is regular feather stitch in white Medici wool.

The top leaf is stitched in satin using light green wool on the top side and medium green wool on the bottom side. The tiny leaves are worked in closed fly using light, medium, and dark green.

The large flower at the top left has shaded chain stitch petals on each side. These are gold on the outer edges, shading to very dark pink towards the inside. The inside of the flower is open cretan stitch in medium blue wool with French knots in three strands of 6-strand yellow cotton scattered within the cretan.

The little bird on the lower right is stitched in blue and yellow wool. The beak is dark yellow wool in satin stitch. The head and breast are yellow long and short stitch with dark yellow satin stitch on the lower breast. The feet are dark rose chain stitch and grasp the branch on which it sits. The eye is a blue wool French knot with dark rose outlining the eye. The top knot is chain stitch in light, medium, and dark blue wool.

The folded wing is in blue wools, starting with satin stitch at the top of the wing. Study the photograph carefully for proper placement of stitches. There follow several rows of chain stitch defining the cap of the wing. The main feathers are buttonhole stitch in light blue wool. The back of the bird is rows of chain stitch with light blue wool on the outside and medium blue next to the wing.

The bird's tail is in feather stitch—imagine that! There are five rows of feather stitch in varying shades of blue, beginning at the tip of the tail and working toward the bottom of the bird.

The flower at the lower left is mainly pink shaded stem stitch. Outline the main shapes of the flower with dark pink wool then fill the shapes with light pink and white wool with stem or outline stitch. The top five oval shapes are in medium and dark yellow fishbone stitch. The base of the flower is medium blue satin stitch. There is a scattering of French knots going up the opening of the flower in light green wool.

The leaf at the base of the heart is worked in shaded chain stitch. Work the main line of the shape in medium olive green chain stitch. There is another line of blue chain stitch in the upper half of the leaf. Fill the top half of the leaf in light green chain and the bottom and the tip with medium green wool.

Little heart-shaped flowers are placed at the top right portion of the heart. The larger one has light pink wool in the middle in fishbone stitch with dark pink satin stitch as the two side petals. The small hearts are worked with dark pink backstitch around the edge. Then work cretan in the backstitches in either white wool or light pink wool. The small leaves are in light green wool fishbone stitch. There is a larger leaf hanging from the top center of the heart, worked in stem stitch with dark green wool down the middle then with rows of lighter green wool stem on each side.

There is a double row of stem stitch in dark and light yellow wool right above the large leaf. Scatter medium blue wool French knots along the yellow line.

FIVE METHODS OF ALTERNATE SHADING

This dainty design uses five methods of shading with chain, stem, French knot, burden, and coral knot stitches.

MATERIALS

Appleton crewel wools: rose #s 144, 146, 148, 752, and 942; green #s 292, 293, and 294; blue #s 741, 742, and 744.

Cream linen twill: 9 x 9 inches (23 x 23 cm)

Chenille needles: two #24

Transfer the design to the linen twill using graphite carbon transfer paper. Use a screw adjustable hoop for all stitches except line stitches, such as stem, outline, and chain, which may be worked soft in the hand.

Using one strand of wool light green, work the top line of the leaf's lower side in coral knot (without using a hoop). Continue working coral knot from right to left, shading from light to dark and using partial rows as necessary. With light green wool work whipped chain at upper edge of leaf. With light blue wool work whipped chain at center vein of leaf. Scatter French knots through the mid portion of leaf, using rose and pinks darker at center and lighter in fringes.

PATTERN ON PAGE 71

To stitch the blossom, work shaded chain on outer petals of flower, first outlining shape with darker pink; then put in dark pink guide lines to define the shape. Fill with shades of pink and rose as in photo. For the center oval portion of flower, lay bars in medium blue wool for burden stitch. Work rows of burden in blues and greens, shading from light blue at top to dark green at bottom. Work edge of oval in outline stitch in medium blue wool. Finish the motif with row of coral knots at the top edge. Scatter French knots at top of oval in rose.

The stems are worked in whipped chain in greens. You may either whip them together or whip the lines separately. The tendril is outline stitch in light green wool. The bottom leaf is stitched in raised stem; lay bars using medium green wool. Work raised stem in medium blue wool down the center; fill from center out using light green on left side and medium green on right side. Both edges of the leaf are darker green. The tip of the leaf is in ordinary stem stitch in medium green. The tendril is worked in whipped outline in light green wool.

Sign (if you wish) and block the finished piece.

TINY TREASURES

Needle Case, Scissors Sheath, & Pin Cushion

Skill level: Beginner

*T*hese *needlework accessories—a scissors sheath, a pin cushion, and a needle case— are suitable for the most delicate chatelaine and are very useful. Whimsical floral designs can be stitched using Appleton crewel wools and six-strand cotton thread on cream linen twill.*

PATTERNS ON PAGE 72

Some of the stitches covered include bullion, twisted chain, satin, crescent spiders, and detached buttonhole arcs. In addition, different finishing methods are discussed and demonstrated. The triangular scissors sheath is made of two separate finished pieces, joined with the fagoting stitch. The square pin cushion is joined with a whipped chain stitch. The oblong needle case is also joined with fagoting, carefully fitted to contain three wooden needle tubes. The finishing methods used are appropriate for use in future projects.

MATERIALS FOR SCISSORS SHEATH

Appleton crewel wools: rose #s 752 and 754' green #s 353 and 355; blue #s 742 and 744; gold #472.

DMC 6-strand cotton: #932 blue

Cream linen twill: 8 x 8 inches (20 x 20 cm)

Lining material

Clear plastic snap closures

Chenille needles: two #24

INSTRUCTIONS FOR SCISSORS SHEATH

Transfer the designs to the linen twill using graphite carbon transfer paper. Use a screw-adjustable hoop for all stitches except line stitches, such as stem, outline, and chain, which may be worked soft in the hand.

Work an open buttonhole stitch on the two tiny triangular flowers in pink wool; space may be left 'between the stitches and then straight stitches of a different color can be added. If desired, additional rows of buttonhole stitches can be worked over the tiny loops made by the original row of buttonhole. These added stitches are made through the wool only and not through fabric.

The little leaves are worked in closed fly stitch using light or medium green wool. All of the stems and branches are worked in outline and whipped outline with medium green wool.

The cluster of three round flowers is worked in crescent spider stitch using blue cotton for the spokes. Whip the spokes with rose wool, then pink wool, and finally blue wool to complete the crescent shape.

All of the flowers at the top of the spray are worked with detached twisted chain stitch. The two round flowers are twisted chain with a common central hole in yellow wool and green wool on the outer edges. The large Queen Ann's Lace flower has lines of blue cotton thread with scattered twisted chain in pink and yellow wool.

FINISHING INSTRUCTIONS FOR SCISSORS SHEATH

After embroidery is complete, cut two of triangle shape in linen twill and also two of triangle shape in lining fabric.

Each side of sheath is lined and finished separately. Sew the long sides of each triangle, right sides together, on machine or by hand. Turn right sides out. Close the short sides of the triangle by folding edges under and blind-stitching together with sewing thread.

Placing the two lined pieces together, lining sides touching, work fagoting stitch along the two long sides using three pieces of 6-strand cotton.

Two pieces of ribbon may be attached at top center for closing the sheath. Or instead a plastic snap closure may be sewn on the inside to keep the scissors in place.

MATERIALS FOR PIN CUSHION

Appleton crewel wools: rose #s 752 and 754' green #s 353 and 355; blue #s 742 and 744; gold #472.

DMC 6-strand cotton: #932 blue

Cream linen twill: 5 x 10 inches (13 x 25 cm)

Stuffing material

Chenille needles: two #24

INSTRUCTIONS FOR PIN CUSHION

Transfer the designs to the linen twill using graphite carbon transfer paper. Use a screw-adjustable hoop for all stitches except line stitches, such as stem, outline, and chain, which may be worked soft in the hand.

Work the wheel buttonhole for two round flowers at the lower right using medium blue wool. If desired, additional rows of buttonhole stitches can be worked over the tiny loops made by the original row of buttonhole. These added stitches are in yellow wool and are made through the wool only and not through fabric. Scatter French knots in yellow wool around the base of the round flowers.

The little leaves are worked in closed fly stitch using light or medium green wool. All of the stems and branches are worked in outline and whipped outline with medium green wool.

The two round flowers are detached twisted chain with a common central hole in medium blue wool and pink wool.

The large central leaf is worked in medium green wool with satin stitch. Place straight stitches within the voids using one strand of blue 6-strand cotton.

FINISHING INSTRUCTIONS FOR PIN CUSHION

After embroidery is complete, work row of chain stitches around all four sides of pin cushion front. Also work row of chain stitches around four sides of pin cushion back. It is important that there be an equal number of chain stitches on each side of the front and of the back.

Cut out the two squares of linen twill, leaving ½ inch (1.2 cm) beyond chain stitches.

Finger press back the ½ inch and place back against front, wrong sides facing. With a long thread in needle, fasten thread and secure front and back together with an overhand whipping motion, working in every chain stitch.

Before whipping the fourth side shut, stuff with filling material (quilt batting or wool roving.)

MATERIALS FOR NEEDLE CASE

Appleton crewel wools: rose #s 752 and 754' green #s 353 and 355; blue #s 742 and 744; gold #472.

DMC 6-strand cotton: #932 blue

Cream linen twill: 9 x 5 inches (23 x 13 cm)

Lining material

3 wooden needle tubes

Clear plastic snap closures

Chenille needles: two #24

Decorative ribbon, optional

INSTRUCTIONS FOR NEEDLE CASE

Transfer the designs to the linen twill using graphite carbon transfer paper. Use a screw-adjustable hoop for all stitches except line stitches, such as stem, outline, and chain, which may be worked soft in the hand.

The butterfly at the top is worked in a combination of chain stitches for the bottom wing and long and short shading for the top two wings, using rose, pink, and yellow wool. The little leaves are worked in closed fly stitch using light or medium green wool. All of the stems and branches are worked in outline and whipped outline with medium green wool.

There are tiny buds worked in detached buttonhole arcs, using pink and rose wool. Refer to the photograph for accurate placement. The large leaf at the top is worked in light green wool using satin stitch. Within the void, place yellow wool French knots.

To the left of the large leaf are three blue bullion rosettes. Use of a long, very narrow needle, such as a beading or milliners needle, may make the bullion knots more easily. At the base of the design is a large flower made entirely of bullion knots, twisted around each other, made of pink, rose, and blue wool.

There are three leaves at the base of the design worked in closed fly stitch in light and medium green. Scatter French knots around these leaves and along the stem at the bottom.

FINISHING INSTRUCTIONS FOR NEEDLE CASE

After embroidery is complete, cut out rectangle shape in linen twill and also rectangle shape in lining fabric.

The needle case is lined and finished. Sew the long sides and top flap of needle holder, right sides together, on machine or by hand. Turn right sides out. Close the bottom of the rectangle by folding edges under and blind-stitching together with sewing thread.

Fold up the bottom of the rectangle, lining sides almost touching. Fit carefully around three wooden needle tubes. Work fagoting stitch along the two sides using three strands of 6-strand cotton.

One or two pieces of ribbon may be added at the top for closure. Sew the plastic snap closure on the inside of flap to keep the wooden needle tubes in place.

CRESCENT IN CREWEL

PATTERN ON PAGE 73

Skill level: Intermediate

This design features subtle shading in a variety of stitches using wools, 6-strand cotton, and #8 pearl cotton. Curves in long and short shading as well as several unusual varieties of spider stitch are explored. Intricate filling patterns are stitched as well as shading with French knots.

MATERIALS

Appleton crewel wools: green #s 353, 403, 405, and 543; blue #s 322 and 324; mauve #s 603 and 605; purple #s 101, 102, 103, and 105; rose burgundy #s142, 145, and 147.

DMC 6-strand cotton: purple, pink, and teal green

DMC #8 pearl cotton: purple

Cream linen twill: 12 x 14 inches (30.5 x 35.5 cm)

Chenille needles: two #24

INSTRUCTIONS

Transfer the design to the linen twill using graphite carbon transfer paper. Use a screw-adjustable hoop for all stitches except line stitches—such as stem, outline, and chain—which may be worked soft in the hand.

All of the major branch is worked in whipped chain using a medium to dark green wool. Smaller stems are worked in whipped outline or whipped stem in light to medium green wool.

The top left arc of the crescent is made up of a ring spider and two crescent spiders which are formed of pink 6-strand cotton plus rose and burgundy crewel wool. The branch also has buds of closed fly worked with pink wool at the tip and medium green wool at the base of each bud.

Ring spider	Crescent spiders
Spokes:	Spokes:
pink 6-strand cotton	pink 6-strand cotton
2 rows: pink 6-strand cotton	2 rows: pink 6-strand cotton
4 rows: rose crewel wool,	3 rows: rose crewel wool
fill with burgundy crewel wool	3 rows: burgundy crewel wool, fill with dark burgundy wool

The lily-like flower is a difficult example of long and short shading in purples. Following the diagram, use the lightest purple at the tips and the darkest purple where the petals overlap. The stamen are worked in whipped back stitch using two strands of a medium purple 6-strand cotton. Scatter a mixture of light and medium teal blue french knots using four strands of 6-strand cotton in the corners where tendrils leave the main stem.

The small, tulip-shaped flower at the lower left has a central petal which has raised chain in the very middle with bars of purple #8 pearl cotton, a central row of raised chain in purple pearl cotton, and then filled on each side with purple wool raised chain. The central petal is defined with outline stitch in purple pearl cotton. This petal has a running stitch on the inside of teal green cotton. It has light purple wool side petals which have been worked in long satin stitches. The satin stitching has then been held down by exaggerated fly stitches. The two lower leaf petals have an outline of green wool worked in stem/outline stitch which has running stitch both inside and outside the leaf. The center of these two leaves is closed fly worked in medium green wool.

The large leaf below is worked in long and short shading, lighter on the outer edges and darkest at the center vein line. (The leaf is worked in light, medium, and dark green wool.)

The central, lower flower is similar to the tulip-shaped flower but has 3 central petals which have raised chain in the very middle with bars of purple #8 pearl cotton, a central row of raised chain in purple pearl cotton, and then filled on each side with purple wool raised chain. The petals are defined with outline stitch in purple pearl cotton and have a running stitch on the inside and outside of teal green cotton. The lower side leaves are worked in long and short stitch using green wools, with lighter outer edges, shading to dark green at the very center. The base of the flower has three closed fly leaves in dark green 6-strand cotton. There is an arcing tendril of medium green wool whipped outline stitch with scattered teal blue cotton french knots.

Several kinds of whipped spider stitches are placed on the tendrils at the lower right side of the crescent. The small round spiders are worked with spokes of pink 6-strand cotton and then whipped with pink, mauve, purple, and burgundy, in quantities to suit the stitcher. The ring spider is worked with similar colors. The tiny leaves are worked in green wool using fly stitch.

The large flower spider could be a challenge in that the spokes are two different sizes in the pattern as shown in the layout. Lay 15 long spokes and 5 short spokes using pink cotton. Work 4 rows of dark purple wool, 2 rows of pink cotton, 5 rows of medium purple wool, 2 rows of green cotton, and fill with lightest purple wool. It will happen that the short spokes are filled before the very long spokes have been filled. In that case simply skip from one set of long spokes to another, on the underneath of the fabric. When all the spokes have been filled, work a row of pink cotton all around all 20 spokes, then work a row of green cotton around the outer edge as well.

At the top right side of the crescent is a flower worked mainly of shaded wool French knots. The outer edge of each petal is dark teal blue wool shaded through light purple to medium purple to dark purple wool at the base of each petal. The three large leaves are worked in light green satin stitch which is held down by dark teal wool fly stitches. The two base leaves are darker green wool stitched in closed fly. The tendril is in whipped outline.

WOODLAND MUSHROOMS

PATTERN ON PAGE 74

Skill level: Intermediate

This design inspired by nature is interpreted into crewel embroidery.

MATERIALS

Appleton crewel wools: purple #s 603 and 605; green #s 353, 354, 355, 344, and 345; coral #s 207, 706, 863, and 864; yellow #s 472, 473, 475, and 841.

DMC Medici crewel wool: beige, tan, and medium green

DMC 6-strand cotton: green #s 3051, 3052, and 3053; coral #945

Cream linen twill: 15 x 15 inches (38 x 38 cm)

Chenille needles: two #24

INSTRUCTIONS

Transfer the designs to the linen twill using graphite carbon transfer paper. Use a screw-adjustable hoop for all stitches except line stitches, such as stem, outline, and chain, which may be worked held in the hand.

Work the fern on the left hand side by stitching the main stem in whipped chain with light green wool. The fronds of the fern are rows of chain with straight stitches out the sides. The oval leaves are worked with satin stitch having each side of the leaves a different color wool. The stems of the leaves are two rows of stem stitch in brown Medici wool, whipped with a different color beige or tan wool. The spiky leaves are worked in shaded stem, combining the green wools and the green cottons. Place a row up the middle in a darker color, either brown or green. The weeds on the right side are several rows of feather stitch using one or two strands of green 6-strand cotton. Also scatter little "pieces" of feather stitches across the piece, using the photograph for placement.

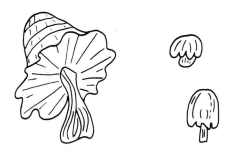

The large mushroom at the left is rather complicated with three separate areas to stitch. The underneath of the cap is a large crescent spider with eleven or twelve very long spokes in coral cotton and then eight or nine short spokes out at the edge of the spider. These short spokes are necessary because the outer edge has curves and because the area between the ends of the long spokes become too large. Whip the spider from the middle stem area using an assortment of yellow and coral wools, such as dark yellow, rust (dark coral), light coral, or medium coral, then fill with light coral; around the outer edge work one row of dark yellow and dark coral.

The top of the cap is long and short shading worked from side to side with rust (dark coral) to medium coral to very light coral. Take care to keep all edges smooth and even.

The stem of the mushroom is worked in chain stitch from top to bottom with division lines in dark coral.

The two little green mushrooms are worked in green and brown wool. The caps are worked in stem and outline stitch in dark greens with brown accents. The stems of the mushrooms are worked in brown satin stitch.

The snail is another example of spider web stitch with the shell being a spiral spider. All stitching is begun at the tiny center of the spiral and is worked all the way out to the edge of the shell. The spokes are laid with coral 6-strand cotton. Whip the spokes with rows of very light coral, light purple, medium coral wools, and coral cotton for the middle; then repeat the color sequence the other way to balance it. The body of the snail is long and short shading in tan and beige Medici wool and light purple wool.

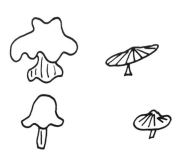

The large mushroom on the right side has a cap worked in curved long and short. The majority of the cap is in light, medium, and dark yellow wool but there are areas of medium coral. Follow the photograph for more accurate color placement. The stem of the mushroom is chain stitch in medium yellow with lines of medium coral.

The medium sized mushroom has a flared cap worked in long and short in shades of dark yellows with medium coral for shading. The stem has two sections. The top section is in dark coral chain stitch worked sideways; the base is medium yellow wool satin stitch.

There are four more tiny mushrooms. Two have caps made up of many French knots and the other two have buttonhole caps. For the caps of French knots use yellow, olive green, and coral for the larger mushroom, and pale yellow, medium yellow, and light green wool for the smaller. The stems of both are worked in satin stitch either in coral or yellow.

The last two tiny mushrooms are stitched in shades of purple using buttonhole stitch. If desired, additional rows of buttonhole stitches can be worked over the tiny loops made by the original row of buttonhole. These added stitches are made through the wool only and not through fabric. The little stems are worked in satin stitch.

BASKET OF THREE-
DIMENSIONAL FLOWERS

PATTERN ON PAGE 75

Skill level: Challenging

This graceful basket is filled with a bouquet of flowers that really are three dimensional. Through a variety of techniques the blossoms stand away from the ground fabric, the butterfly's wing seems perched ready for flight, and the basket itself is heavily textured.

MATERIALS

Appleton crewel wools: blue #s 742, 744, and 746; green #s 353 and 355; mint green #431.

DMC Medici crewel wool: white and pale blue

DMC 6-strand cotton: white; blue #797

DMC #8 pearl cotton: blue #s 800 and 809; green #368

Cream plain weave linen: 15 x 15 inches (38 x 38 cm)

Plastic "bone" rings

White and clear rocaille beads, optional

Navy blue bugle beads, optional

Chenille needles: two #24 and one #18

INSTRUCTIONS

Transfer the design to the plain weave linen using graphite carbon transfer paper. Use a screw-adjustable hoop for all stitches except line stitches, such as stem, outline, and chain, which may be worked held in the hand.

The branch of three flowers on the right side has three leaves worked in trellis stitch with green #8 pearl cotton. The stem is also stitched in green pearl cotton in a whipped chain stitch. The flowers are in a loose satin stitch worked with three pieces of light blue wool, following the direction lines on the line drawing. Then work detached buttonhole stamen with medium blue #8 pearl cotton. If desired, place a white rocaille bead at the end of the stamen.

The spray of flowers immediately above those in figure A have a stem in mint green wool worked in stem stitch with leaves of single detached chains (lazy daisy stitch.) The flowers are raised cup stitch in blue #8 pearl cotton. The stamen in this case are dark blue cotton long bullion knots that go from the flower center to the outside of the blossom.

The tulip-shaped flowers at the top center of the basket each have a central section worked of raised close herringbone with 3 pieces of light blue wool in the needle at the same time. The flower sides are dark blue wool in slanted satin stitch. The stems are dark green wool stem stitch and there are French knots in dark blue cotton scattered along the tendrils and placed at the top of each flower. The large leaf below the flowers is slanted satin in dark green wool.

The flower at the center has three detached petals; they are worked in detached cretan stitch petal on paper with dark blue cotton chain stitch and filled with white and pale blue Medici wool cretan stitch. Since your detached petals will improve with practice, be sure to practice this stitch several times if it's new to you. Work the chain stitches small and evenly for the best result. The base of the flower is medium blue wool satin stitch. The leaves at the base of this flower are satin stitch in light green wool.

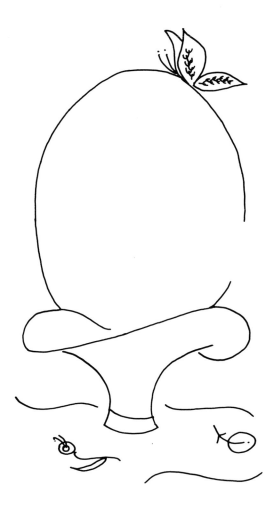

The spray of flowers on the left has stems and tendrils of green #8 pearl cotton and the leaves are closed fly stitch also with the green pearl cotton. There are french knots in dark blue cotton scattered along the tendrils. The flowers are detached buttonhole rings in medium blue #8 pearl cotton which are twisted in a bow shape and then tacked onto the fabric. If desired, you may place three clear rocaille beads at the top of each flower or you can stitch light blue French knots.

There is a spray of three flowers hanging over the edge of the basket worked in light, medium, and dark blue. They are worked in detached buttonhole rings over plastic bone rings. If desired, a dark blue bugle bead can be placed on each ring as a stamen. The stem for these three is mint green wool in stem stitch.

The basket base is ceylon stitch in white Medici wool. The top rim of the basket is a large chain stitch using two pieces of light blue #8 pearl cotton together with two pieces of dark blue wool, together in the needle. The bottom edge of the basket base is raised chain on a bar with the same four pieces of thread in the needle. The handle of the basket is heavy chain braid, using blue and white 6-strand cotton plus 2 pieces each of light blue wool and dark blue wool; you will need to use a much larger needle.

Stitch the lines beneath the basket in mint green wool. Two blossoms have fallen from the bouquet, one raised cup stitch, and one buttonhole over plastic ring.

The back wings of the butterfly are stitched in chain with green #8 pearl cotton. The body is also chain in green pearl cotton and the antennae are long straight stitches in one strand of 6-strand cotton. Place feather stitches within the wings. The top wing of the butterfly is free standing over wire (see stitch instructions).

CREWEL WITH NEEDLELACE

PATTERN ON PAGE 76

Skill level: Challenging

Crewel embroidery and needlelace combine in this piece with exquisite results. Using stitches such as ceylon, cretan, raised cup, and buttonhole variations creates depth and texture not usually found in crewel embroidery. The needlelace is worked in wool and blends with the traditional embroidery stitches.

MATERIALS

Appleton crewel wools: sky blue #s 561, 563, and 564; cornflower blue #s 461, 462, and 463; green #s 353, 354, and 356; dull green #s 291, 292, and 293; bright mauve #s 451, 452, and 453; rose #s 144 and 146.

DMC 6-strand cotton: pink #605; aqua #518; purple #209; blue #809

Linen twill: 15 x 15 inches (38 x 38 cm)

Chenille needles: two #24

INSTRUCTIONS

Transfer the designs to the linen twill using graphite carbon transfer paper. Use a screw-adjustable hoop for all stitches except line stitches, such as stem, outline, and chain, which may be worked held in the hand.

All of the major branch is worked in whipped chain using a medium green wool. Smaller stems are worked in whipped outline or whipped stem in light to medium green wool.

The flower at the upper left has a crescent spider at its top. Lay spokes with pink 6-strand cotton. Then whip with an assortment of rose and green wool and with blue 6-strand cotton. The tendrils are two strands of 6-strand blue cotton in a whipped back stitch. It also has seven detached petals; they are worked in detached cretan stitch petal on paper.

For petals 1 through 4 work with pink cotton work chain stitch and fill with light rose wool cretan stitch. For petals 5, 6, and 7 work the chain in aqua cotton and fill with the same light rose wool for the cretan stitch. Since your detached petals will improve with practice, be sure to practice this stitch several times if it's new to you. Work the chain stitches small and evenly for the best result. The petals are attached to the fabric in the order numbered on the diagram. Simply tie the threads together on the back of the fabric in the appropriate place.

The spray of flower buds at the upper left are worked in closed fly stitch in two colors: a flower color at the tip and green at the base. Use light and medium sky blue wool for the tips and green wool at the base. Place the lighter buds near the top and darker ones lower down.

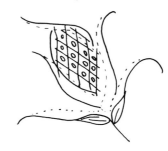

The large lily flower on the lower left is worked in a combination of chain and detached buttonhole stitch. First work the laid trellis filling with green wool as the trellis and tying with blue cotton; then place a detached chain with one strand of blue 6-strand cotton within each diamond. Next work the petals in the order noted. For each petal you will work several rows of chain stitch in blues, corresponding to the shape in the diagram. Then using either a blue or a mauve wool and a very long thread in the needle, work detached buttonhole from the base of the petal to the tip and then back again. Don't pierce the fabric but only pick up one loop of the chain stitch. On succeeding rows only pick up the loops of the buttonhole stitch. It is difficult to keep the stitches even but don't become discouraged. By working the petals in order, they will overlap one another.

The two small leaves at the base of this flower are worked in medium green wool in closed fly stitch after all other work on the flower is finished.

The large leaf below the lily flower is stitched in grey green in slanted satin stitch. Take care to ensure a smooth edge on each side of the sections. Down the central void place a row of outline stitch with 2 strands of pink 6-strand cotton. Next to that put a row of running stitch using 1 piece of aqua 6-strand cotton.

The pomegranate flower at the bottom center also has a laid trellis filler which must be worked first. Using the picture as a guide to size, lay the trellis in dark rose wool and tie it with three strands of pink 6-strand cotton. Then work a French knot in each diamond using pink cotton and rose wool in the needle at the same time.

Work interlaced buttonhole in light, medium, and dark sky blue wool. The first row of stitches will begin on the outer left side of the shape and the stitches will pierce the fabric along the outer edge. This is the only row that pierces the fabric; subsequent rows will pick up the bar of the previous row. Work only one half of the shape at a time. Recognize that some of the trellis will be covered by interlaced buttonhole. When that is completed then turn the work upside down and make another half on the other side. When this step is completed, work outline stitch completely around the shape to neaten the edges.

The leaves at the top and bottom of the shape are worked in closed fly stitch using light, medium, and dark green.

There are two large leaves at the bottom right which are worked in slanted satin stitch in grey green wool, light,

medium, and dark. Down the central void is a line of French knots made from three-stranded purple cotton.

The spray of flower buds on the right side is worked mostly in raised cup stitch in light, medium, and dark mauve wool. The French knots in the centers are worked in pink cotton. There is one flower which is worked in buttonhole stitch using medium mauve wool. If desired, additional rows of buttonhole stitches can be worked over the tiny loops made by the original row of buttonhole stitches. These added stitches are made through the wool only and not through fabric. Then place a few French knots using pink cotton. The tiny leaves are worked in closed fly with medium green wool.

The bluebell flowers are worked with ceylon stitch which resembles knitting when completed. Beginning at the X marked on the diagram and using the darkest cornflower blue, work ceylon stitch. Note that this stitch is always worked from the same side; there are long carry-over stitches on the back of the fabric. Take care not to pierce the fabric when stitching but to only work through the previous row of loops. It will take about 20 rows to complete the shape. Shade from dark through medium to light blue. As you reach the end of the shape you will notice that the lip of the flower curls up, much as knitting does. Work outline stitch around the rim in lightest blue. Place long arm French knots in pink, aqua, and purple cotton, using only one strand of 6-strand cotton, coming from within the bluebell and extending over the rim. See photograph.

The base of the flower is worked after completion of the above. Work two closed fly leaves in light green at the base of each. Then work two large leaves in light green wool using slanted satin stitch.

GALLERY

*Inspiration evolves from a dream or a vision of a design worthy of portrayal
in the medium of embroidery. This vision is studied and pondered by the artist,
awake and asleep. The inspired design is rendered on paper in
assorted variations until the artist is satisfied that the rendering
does justice to the vision. Choices of stitch and thread
are added to the elements of design that have to be considered
when finalizing the product. The technical skills and innate talents
of the artist are used to develop the original dream into a workable design
in embroidery. This explanation of inspiration relates in sterile terms
the creation of a work of art. What it does not address are the difficulties
that surround this process. Surmounting these difficulties serves to strengthen
the artist's work. Things that come easy often do not result in excellence.
Further, a work of art results from constant striving for faultless excellence.
The pages that follow showcase the works of traditional, contemporary,
and innovative artists, all of whom have achieved that excellence.*

MARJORIE L. JONES

Eve's Apple

Marj is a well-respected teacher of crewel embroidery who has influenced many stitchers in the Eastern half of the United States, and she often uses this piece for demonstration when teaching workshops. It features a whipped spider shaded lengthwise in terra cotta shades to shape the pomegranate. Notice the use of voids to achieve light and airy leaves with a lace filling stitch. Blue French knots on a stalk contribute another bit of color to this design.

MARY-DICK DIGGS

Untitled

Mary-Dick began embroidering at the age of 4½, and she has studied under some of the foremost teachers of the 20th century: Josephine Jardine, Muriel Baker, Peg Lunt, Mildred Davis, Jo Bucher, and Grace O'Neill. "All of them were true teachers—giving, sharing, and eliciting the best from their students by their own joy in what they were doing. How fortunate I am to have had such examples!" This piece is on blue British satin. One of the shells has multiple bands of color worked in whipped spider stitch; another has a pearl peeking out.

MARJORIE L. JONES

Oriental Iris

This large, over-the-mantle piece in wool and silk on celadon green satin was designed by Marj and inspired by an embroidery viewed on a trip to England. Virginia Podufaly of Chestertown, Maryland, stitched the iris to duplicate the prize flowers in her garden. The silk frog, snail, and butterflies add a touch of whimsy to this chinoserie design.

MARJORIE L. JONES

Oriental Roundel

The Bonsai branch and tree peony motif give this design its feeling of the Orient. Crewel wools and touches of silk on the little bird achieve a naturalistic effect. The peony petals are also directionally shaded for the illusion of depth and dimension.

Long silk bullion knots add a touch of drama to the golden chrysanthemum and the lavender wisteria. The wisteria also uses a detached chain stitch for subtle shading. These flowers combine to create the look of an antique porcelain plate.

JAN MOHS

Baby Robin

Trasferring the design is an important part of the process for Jan, and she uses several methods. One method is to first make a reverse drawing on a very thin fabric with a permanent marker. She then places this design sheet under the ground fabric and bastes through both layers to create the design on the right side. In another method Jan uses a pencil drawing on washed muslin to baste on the design. "At any point I can change the design by simply unstitching (picking out) the basted running stitches."

HELEN LAUER

Helen's Masterpiece

This piece was designed by Betsy Leiper, a friend of Helen's who incorporated Helen's passion for purple into the design. Many of the motifs are adaptations from 17th- and 18th-century crewel pieces, and this piece taught Helen to really enjoy stitching animals.

Traditional Crewel I

Pat Allen believes she was drawn to crewel embroidery because of its creative possibilities. She finds the lovely curves of stems and tendrils fascinating. Pat studied at the Wallingford Crewel Studio in Pennsylvania, and in England at the Royal School of Needlework and at The Embroiderers' Guild in Hampton Court. She has a strong interest in the presentation of traditional designs and feels that her strengths lie in her preparation and attention to detail.

The pieces shown here were designed as a pair to showcase the beautiful texture of raised chain bars, Palestrina knots, and French knots in contrast to shaded outline, shaded chain, and soft shading. There are more than 38 shades of colors in the designs. Some of the shades are simply accents that are repeated for a good balance of color, while others represent the gradation of color needed for shading.

Traditional
Crewel II

MARY-DICK DIGGS

Prim
and Proper

"Over the years I have encountered two types of embroidery personalities. One type needs the security of the grid; they prefer counted embroidery and find surface stitchery intimidating. The other type finds the grid limiting and loves the freedom of surface work. How wonderful that today's world of embroidery has room and challenges for both."

There are two types of leaves in wool, one a sort of or nue, the other a split stitch shading. The bouquet is in a pot made of woven ribbon stitched over with pearl cotton. The background is pulled thread. This is one of the few examples where crewel embroidery works well on canvas, and that is because the stitching of crewel requires unlimited opportunities to insert the needle into the background fabric. When one is working on a wide open mesh, stitching crewel becomes more difficult.

PAT ALLEN

Petticoat Pocket

This original, traditional-style design was worked in Appleton crewel yarns on cream linen twill fabric. As in early crewelwork, a variety of stitches were used, including shaded French knots, outline, chain, pekinese, seed, and chevron stitch. The title comes from the petticoat pockets worn for more than 300 years beneath the skirt, behind an apron, or over a skirt by women who needed a place to keep valuables.

CONTEMPORARY

AUDREY FRANCINI

Birds of
the World

Shown here is one panel from a
set of three stitched by Audrey
It features a crested crane, a
least green bittern, and an arctic
tern, and is worked in both flat
and twisted Japanese silk.

AUDREY FRANCINI

Chanticleer

This piece was worked in Japanese silk.
The tail feathers are two colors of silk
twisted together to create an iridescent
effect, while the comb and wattle are
clusters of Japanese knots.

JO-ANN JENKINS

The Challenge:
My Secret Garden

"My embroidery designs are inspired by nature and the countryside," says Jo-Ann. When she sees a moss-covered rock on a walk in the woods, her husband laughs and says, "I know, French knots." She develops ideas for stitches and colors from her observations of nature, collecting and sketching specimens, and then matching them for color with six-stranded embroidery cottons. Jo-Ann started this piece in the early summer so that she would have the flowers available for matching colors and shapes.

Jo-Ann Jenkins

Swindon

Delightful flower vines border this scene of nature which was inspired by the artist's visit to Swindon, England where she spent a few days sharing a garden with a wren, a flock of blue tits, and hedgehogs! To set off the central portion, Jo-Ann wrapped thin pieces of fiberglass material with silk threads from a weaver. The stitches are mainly long and short with some soft shading, closed fly, buttonhole and French knots.

MARNIE RITTER

Embroidered Iris Sofa

As long as Marnie Ritter has been involved with needleart, flowers and their shapes have intrigued her. Her interest in this design source probably developed from the time she spent as a child in her father's flower shop. This early experience also served as her introduction to art. She began stitching at about six years old and still enjoys the flower shapes best. Marnie enjoys the challenge of trying new combinations of skills and is always looking toward the next idea to inspire her.

MARNIE RITTER

Iris and Butterfly Picture

Marnie used the iris pattern from the sofa on page 92 to create a totally different look. To prepare the background, the iris was transfer painted onto a canvas mesh, given a Japanese paper application, and then gilded. The iris and butterfly were then stitched with silk thread.

Susan Dawson

Basket of Apples

Sue was taught to embroider in the early 1960s by neighbors who thought her mother was neglecting her education as a female child. Her teachers wanted her to follow traditions and follow the lines, while Sue wanted to explore the space and colors. The lessons didn't last very long. Sue was an adult before she understood that she had to master technique in order to really be able to express herself well and produce a satisfying quality of work. The piece shown here is an example of excellence in long and short stitch.

CAROL ALGIE HIGGINBOTHAM

Winter's Glory

When beginning a project, Carol usually decides what type of general idea she wants in the piece and then puts it aside for a while. "Usually," she says, "the design concept will be in my mind when I start to work on the project." Carol is an exquisite stitcher who is another devotee of traditional Japanese silk embroidery. The piece shown here represents the Christmas holiday in its secular aspect with poinsettias, Christmas roses, and holly.

PAMELA SCHOLZ

Hawaiian Orchid Show

After many years of selling her paintings professionally, the process had become drudgery. Seeking to expand her boundaries and to avoid this artistically lethal state of mind, Pamela Scholz began working in fiber art several years ago. The piece shown here was inspired during a tour of the islands. The boulders were constructed from thickly padded denim appliques highlighted with a thin wash of acrylic paint and were further shaped with stitching to create crevices and bulges in the rock. Tree fern fronds were done in needleweaving so they would stand out from the background. Some of the leaves were made over an armature made of wire while others were cut from UltraSuede and tacked down to resemble clumps of foliage.

Pamela Scholz

Mango Hummingbirds

Pamela concentrates on one piece until it is finished. She can't stand to leave it alone until it is complete, even when the kitchen floor is so dirty that it sticks to the bottom of her feet! Pamela likes to use silk and lightweight denim because of the varied textures in which they come. As the areas being worked advance toward the foreground, Pamela elevates them farther and farther above the ground material. She uses several techniques to do this: multiple layers of stitches worked over each other, padded applique, needleweaving around a wire form, wrapping thread around a piece of shaped cardboard, or needlelace.

JUDY JEROY

Woodland Path

Follow a woodland path to a scene of delight! Realistic flowers in soft shading and cretan-stitched weeds are part of the vista. The void in the center of the piece suggests a path wandering through the scene. "I felt it was important to continue the illusion of the path by painting areas on the mat with more grasses and weeds," explains Judy.

JUDY JEROY

Butterfly Path

For this piece, the artist applied an extensive application of dyes to create two colors of green to simulate background foliage. Rocks and grasses line the edges of a voided area to suggest a path, while a resting butterfly was worked in long and short shading using stranded cotton.

JUDY JEROY

Vernal Sunrise

The addition of surface stitchery to a drawing on muslin fabric, enhanced by a background colored by crayons, offers a way to stretch embroidery. After coloring the fabric, a hot iron over paper towels was used to set the crayon and to remove the wax.

JUDY JEROY

Carolina Wrens

In this work an entire branch of leaves and flowers was painted with acrylics, while the stitching concentrates on the wrens. Close study of bird photographs was important to stitch them accurately. Portions of leaves and flowers have been further embellished with stitches.

JUDY JEROY

Great Blue Herons

"The first time I was challenged to devise a major design, I envisioned a view of waterfowl in a wetland setting. The difficulty of portraying a vast amount of water in stitchery was daunting. It finally occurred to me that the solution was to color the fabric in the water area. So, without instruction from anyone, I experimented with acrylic paints on wet and on dry linen twill. The results were marginally successful. That is, the area that was painted became slightly stiffer than the surrounding areas and more difficult to stitch. On the other hand, the design was planned so that the stitching only occurred in two major areas—the herons—with the rest of the stitching relatively sparse. Careful attention was paid to the "make up" on the birds' faces in order to give life and expression to them."

JUDY JEROY

Sunset Emotions

The lavish use of paint and dyes to embellish plain cream muslin needs very little stitchery to achieve its purpose. Color washes were used to show the sunset, sand, grasses, and the coming storm. Windblown trees were stitched by hand and by machine. The grasses are windblown, bending in the path of the storm-pushed rain. The couple walking on the sand are shown only as silhouettes, and were done in pen.

Audrey Francini

Woodland Awakening

Audrey has an extensive background in drawing and oil painting, which is an incredible asset when blending yarn colors to achieve realistic effects. This piece was worked mostly in Appleton wool with the trillium, hepatica, and dog-toothed violet stitched in *au Ver a Soie*.

JO-ANN JENKINS

Woodland Plate

The Town & Country Mouse, a children's book by Jan Brett, inspired Jo-Ann for this piece. The design has a wonderfully heavy base made from stitched mosses, stones, and grass. Many of Jo-Ann's floral designs are inspired by the fresh-cut flowers that she presses and collects.

CAROL A. WILLIAMS

Trees

For this piece, Carol envisioned a path she could control with light, so she searched for photographs to enhance that thought. Most of the piece is stitched with very little of the plain painted background showing. (The same embroidery process used for Window with a View was used here.) The small pale area on the left is void of stitches except for a few metallic and rayon threads to add shine and interest. Most of her stitches are straight stitches (similar to painting), but the area around the open view was done in French knots.

CAROL A. WILLIAMS

My Secret Garden

For this piece, Carol wanted to remember happier times, so she chose the idea of her mother in a garden that she would have loved. Carol started with a green, marbleized canvas, which she further embellished with painting. Carol stitched the face with stranded silk, and then created leaves from fabric and handmade paper to add a dimensional effect. The leaves were then stitched to the base to enforce the idea of looking through a thickly wooded area.

CAROL A. WILLIAMS

Window with a View

In designing this piece, Carol chose a view that she personally had never seen, the West, but which she would LIKE to see. So her answer was a view of a wish. She worked with tracing paper, colored pencils, and watercolor markers to set up her basic idea. The design was then transferred to a cotton fabric background cloth that takes water-based paint well and the material was stretched. Next, the sky was painted and left as is to achieve a distant effect. The rest of the picture was also painted. Then, using an iron-on process, she placed pieces of printed cotton over the painted ground and stitched over them.

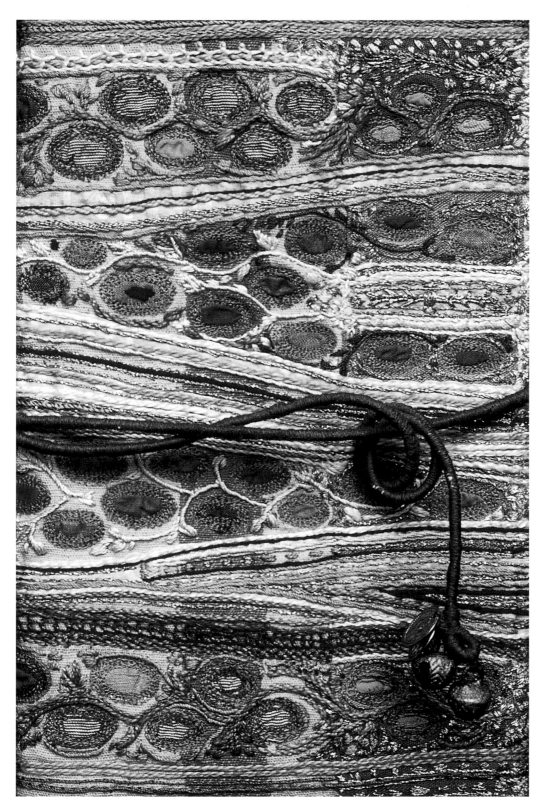

JAN KOZICKI

Metamorphosis Series #2: Sketch Book Cover - Seeds of Thoughts and Sights

Jan keeps a sketch book for design ideas, and the visual image from the following entry was so intense that she wanted—and needed—to create a cover for her sketch book. "On the streams that flow through my head thoughts and sights

float like pregnant seeds seeking the light of creativity." She also loved the idea, and the luxury, of being able to keep on holding and enjoying an embroidered piece. The cover is worked using machine applique and hand embroidery in cotton, linen, metallic, silk, and viscose threads on cotton fabric.

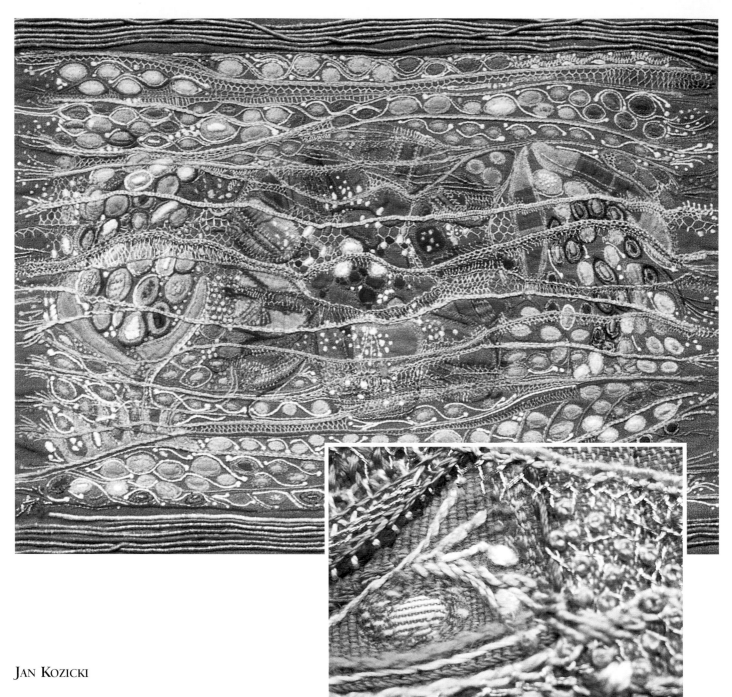

Jan Kozicki

Metamorphosis Series #1:
Seed Cycle

Jan has a background in painting and design, but she finds herself captivated by the magic in fabric, threads, and stitches. She uses a myriad of tiny stitches to create her embroidered pieces. This piece is a fabric collage using machine appliqué and hand embroidery; it measures 20 x 22 inches.

Jan Kozicki

My Cherry Orchard. My Dacha

In this work, Jan continues her love of over-all designs that have many centers of interest. The glow of the threads satisfies her love of brocade, without the work of weaving it! The piece is machine embroidery on cotton with silk, viscose, and metallic threads; it measures 10¼ x 11½ inches.

Self Portrait at Forty

To India Hayford, surface embroidery is a form of meditation and prayer. Her stitchery is an exploration of the world, of her own mind, and the feminine principles that guide her life. The original idea for this piece was a silhouette decorated in the rustic fabrics and rough beads that she thought best represented her. The exotic part of her personality emerged as she rejected raw clay beads and denim in favor of sequins and velour and satin. The charms hanging from the bead strings and earrings represent people and important things in her life.

Waterfall

India experiments freely with new stitches, a variety of ground fabrics, and the fascinating realm of texture via both thread and stitch variety. This piece was an experiment in carrying embroidery beyond the boundaries of traditional space. The cascade spills into a loose shower of threads that sway in the wind and add movement as well as dimension. It is now mounted onto an asymmetrical base, freeing the scene from the confines of a traditional rectangle.

BUCKY KING

Big Horn Mountain

Bucky King was a pioneer in the pursuit of creative expression and excellence in embroidery, and was instrumental in the formation of the National Standards Council of American Embroiderers (since renamed the Council of American Embroiderers). This piece is an example of how she uses traditional techniques in different ways. Water color and torn paper segments are held together with silk thread in irregular long and short stitch.

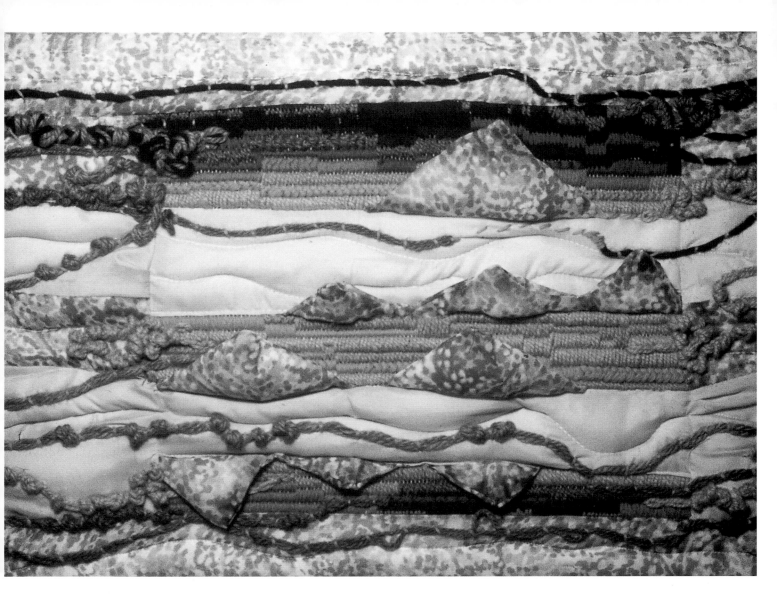

BUCKY KING

Water

Bucky lives in rural America, and all of her design inspiration comes from the environment in which she lives. This piece was done on mixed ground fabrics in surface stitchery and appliqué using wool, cotton, and silk threads.

CASEY BRADFORD

Rock Garden: A Study in Textures

Casey is fascinated with texture, and she loves to combine hand and machine embroidery in which there are endless possibilities of techniques and effects. This piece has lots of threads and lots of different stitches to represent the various rocks and foliage.. Some knitting and weaving threads are used, as well as wools and pearl cottons. The stitches range from feather and buttonhole clumps to bullion and palestrina knots.

Casey Bradford

Brigadoon

This piece is actually a combination of hand and machine stitchery. The layers of the ground and grass were created wtih a machine cutwork technique. The pieces were cut apart after stitching, fringed, applied to a background fabric with sheers and overlays. Hand embellishment was done with pearl cottons in straight stitch, buttonhole clumps, and French knots, both tight and loose. Casey wanted this piece to float off the background and appear ephemeral, as if it, like the town of Brigadoon, might only appear in a place one day every 100 years.

KATHERINE COLWELL

Juniper

Having lived much of the last 27 years in isolated locations or remote communities (her husband is retired from the U.S. Forest Service), Katherine has always felt a kinship with adaptations Colonial stitchers made in their lives and with their stitching. The early American habit of individualizing crewel patterns and designs with personal motifs is something with which she has always connected. Katherine has been drawing and stitching trees since 1971 when she took her first drawing class. In her words: "It's possible to say my life is in the trees." This piece measures 2⅜ x 2½ inches.

KATHERINE COLWELL

Brown's Point Aspen

Brown's Point Aspen is one of four images in a larger work entitled *Bliss of Growth*. The four tree images which comprise Bliss of Growth use freely worked long and short stitches, sometimes layered, to achieve just the right blended effect of colors and threads. The trees include fir, aspen, juniper, and an orchard. This piece measures 2⅛ x 2½ inches.

MAUREEN PRATT

Around the Seasons

Although Maureen Pratt learned to stitch as a child, she didn't really begin serious stitching until college, when she was a textiles and clothing major. Later she spent several years as a horticulturist working in an arboretum. Having spent so many years gardening, visiting, reading, and talking about gardens, they are a natural choice of subject matter for her. Maureen usually draws thumbnail sketches to decide the placement of important features, but most of the drawing is done with her needle and thread.

MAUREEN PRATT

All Work and Play Too

The outside of this piece measures 6 x 7¾ inches, and contains fragments of all the chores in Maureen's garden. These scenes form a frame around the inside image of Maureen relaxing on the lounge after the chores are finished with a book in her lap and the dog at her feet. The stitches used are chain, satin, straight, feather, and French knots, and the ground fabric is upholstery-weight cotton. Stranded cotton and metallic threads were used.

Helenn Rumpel

Window to the East

Helenn Rumpel is an internationally recognized fiber artist. This piece was chosen to receive a Merit Award at the 14th National Exhibit of the Embroiderers' Guild of America. Helenn pays special attention to innovative presentation and framing, making sure that frames (when used) relate specifically to accentuate the piece they hold. The piece was framed in an old Russian traditional wooden frame whose ornate design relates directly to the stitchery held within.

HELENN RUMPEL

St. Michael and Troika

Helenn's special interest in creative needlework began to develop 25 years ago and has continued to grow and expand. In *St. Michael*, shown left, St. Michael is presented from a contemporary point of view, but in an old, carved Mexican bowl with a Spanish sun sign above the stitchery.

Luke 1:9-15

Gayle Williamson began with kits back in the 1970s. In recent years she has shifted to spiritual and religious imagery in her art, predominantly framed scenes of angels, Madonnas, and other figures created entirely from stitchery patterns. Gayle believes art has a healing effect and volunteers regularly at a Christian Mission shelter in Louisville to help the women and to give her own efforts a new sense of purpose.

Hagar

Gayle's travels to Europe and Indonesia, as well as her study of Renaissance art, have served as inspiration for her work. She describes her art as "giving freedom, grace, transformation, and redemption a modern voice. Collectively, my work is a battle or a stand against evil."

Holy, Holy, Holy

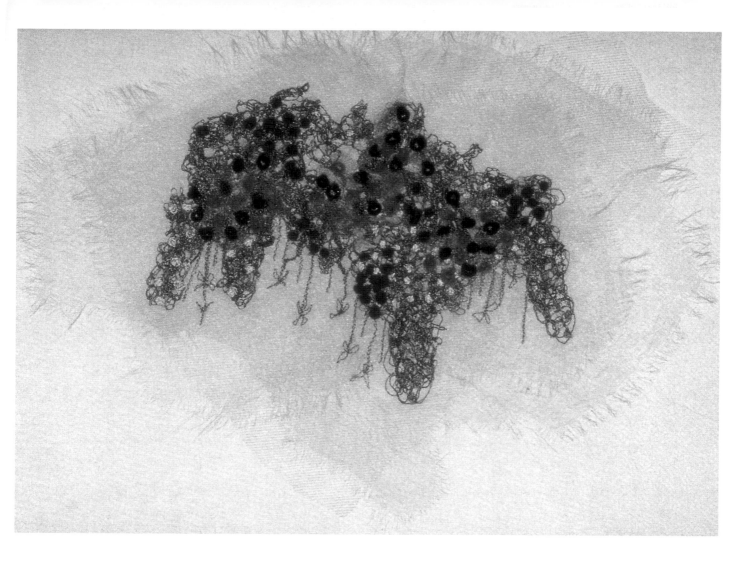

CASEY BRADFORD

Impressionist Garden

This piece is made from background stitches on water-soluble fabric that was rinsed, dried, applied to cotton fabric, and then layered with chiffon. This "background" was then embellished with hand-stitched flowers using chenille threads in French knots. Little bits of tulle were then tied in to create texture and add color.

INDEX